DR. PAUL COSTA

Healing THE MULTITUDES

HEALING & DELIVERANCE MADE SIMPLE

© 2015 Paul Costa
HEALING THE MULTITUDES
HEALING AND DELIVERANCE MADE SIMPLE
Printed in the USA

ISBN (Print Edition): 978-0-9963594-0-5

ISBN (Kindle): 978-0-9963594-1-2

ISBN (eBook): 978-0-9963594-2-8

Library of Congress Control Number: 2015906743

Prepared for publication by: www.palmtreeproductions.com

All Rights Reserved. This book is protected by the copyright laws of the United States of America. This book may not be copied or reprinted for commercial gain or profit. The use of short quotations is permitted. Permission will be granted upon request. The author guarantees all contents are original and do not infringe upon the legal rights of any other person or work.

Scripture quotations are taken from THE HOLY BIBLE, NEW INTERNATIONAL VERSION®, NIV® Copyright © 1973, 1978, 1984, 2011 by Biblica, Inc.® Used by permission. All rights reserved worldwide.

TO CONTACT THE AUTHOR:
WWW.PAULCOSTAMINISTRY.COM
email: spaulcosta@gmail.com

Dedication

To my wife, Jan, my best friend and the love of my life.

Acknowledgement

Special thanks to Dr. Daniel K. Madsen, a man of God who heard the Holy Spirit and kindly responded.

WHAT OTHERS ARE SAYING

Paul Costa has written what I believe is the most knowledgeable and revelatory book on healing and deliverance I have yet encountered. He has simplified the complex issues of Christian faith in action and the authority of the believer at work to heal disease and cast out demons. *Healing the Multitudes* is a practical training manual for all Christians to be able to operate in the ministry of healing and deliverance in their everyday lives. No elite club, no rites of passage, no gimmicks—just faith working and miracles manifesting.

I have read many books on healing and deliverance and this one is exceptional. Reading each chapter is like examining a diamond, many-faceted and brilliant. Paul provides sound scriptural interpretation, practical examples, and powerful testimonies. *Healing the Multitudes* is a fountain of faith to drink from and an edification emersion of revelation.

JOHN P. KELLY
ICAL— International Coalition of Apostolic Leaders
LEAD—Leadership Education for Advancement & Development

Healing the Multitudes will open your eyes and heart to the truth concerning your healing and the healing of others. This book is a gift filled with Scripture, knowledge, and practical application on how you will bring healing to those around you.

Paul's passion for healing and deliverance is evident as you read his life experiences. I highly recommend this information to everyone who has a heart to give and to serve.

RON DEPRIEST
World Impact Network

Paul Costa is a unique man—an astute student and disciple of Christ. As a "gentle giant" from the N.F.L. with a degree in English Literature, he has crafted a primer on the practicalities and how to's of fulfilling a ministry and gift of prayer for those needing both physical and spiritual healing.

Healing the Multitudes is well written, clear, and compelling. It helps remove many of our excuses for not believing God for healing, or expecting that healing ministries are for only a few "special" believers.

DENNIS PEACOCKE
Strategic Christian Services

CONTENTS

1	Chapter 1	God's Primary Strategy
21	Chapter 2	Give it Away
35	Chapter 3	It's All God
59	Chapter 4	Commissioned, Commanded, Empowered
77	Chapter 5	Just Do It
97	Chapter 6	Forget the Failures
109	Chapter 7	Deliverance and Healing
127	Chapter 8	The Enemy Wants You
139	Chapter 9	Keep it Simple
161	Chapter 10	Persistence
177	Chapter 11	The Will of God
189	Chapter 12	Let's Have Revival

211 Appendix A
   TESTIMONIES
221 Appendix B
   PAUL COSTA'S TESTIMONY
231 About the Author
   MEET PAUL COSTA

Chapter One

God's Primary Strategy

When Jesus came to the earth, did the Godhead have a specific plan in mind to be carried out? Yes, of course! Was anything left to chance, like the shifting of a sand dune? No! Like everything Jesus did, there was a purpose, as when he began his ministry with a specific model as described in Matthew 4:23-25:

> ... preaching the good news of the Kingdom, and healing every disease and sickness among the people. News about him spread all over Syria, and people brought to him all who were ill with various diseases, those suffering severe pain, the demon-possessed, those having seizures, and the paralyzed; and he healed them. Large crowds from Galilee, the Decapolis, Jerusalem, Judea and the region across the Jordan followed him.

Then after Jesus chose his twelve apostles, and spent time with them, he sent them out to the various towns and villages and instructed them to carry out the same model of ministry:

2 | Healing the Multitudes

> *... he gave them power and authority to drive out all demons and to cure diseases, and he sent them out to preach the Kingdom of God and to heal the sick.*
>
> LUKE 9:1-2

The first thing Jesus told the apostles when he met them was that he would make them fishers of men. When he sent them, he specifically sent them with the most important strategy in the New Testament for bringing in a harvest of souls and planting the church. He wanted to make sure they were successful in fishing for souls.

The second group Jesus sent out were the seventy-two. When he sent this group to the towns and villages, he sent them with the same message and the same model of ministry:

> *Heal the sick who are there and tell them, "The Kingdom of God has come near you."*
>
> LUKE 10:9

The group of seventy-two were all novices and a completely different group from the twelve apostles who were sent out by Jesus:

> *The seventy-two returned with joy and said, "Lord, even the demons submit to us in your name."*
>
> LUKE 10:17

Until they were sent out, the seventy-two never experienced having authority over demons, so they were somewhat surprised when the demons submitted to them.

The next (third) group Jesus sends out includes all believers—encompassing all of Christian history through the present:

"Go into all the world and preach the Gospel to all creation. Whoever believes and is baptized will be saved, but whoever does not believe will be condemned. And these signs will accompany those who believe: '… they will place their hands on sick people, and they will get well.'"

MARK 16:15-18

To summarize the primary strategy of Jesus:

- Jesus, himself, used healing/teaching and healing as his model of ministry.

- Jesus sent his twelve apostles and had them use the same model of ministry.

- Jesus sent a larger group of seventy-two, and told them to use the same model of ministry

- Jesus then sends all Christians throughout all of history, and tells us to use that same model of ministry.

Why? So we can show the world the power of the Holy Spirit with its signs, wonders, and miracles, and validate the Gospel. This is Jesus' basic strategy to change the world.

To plant a church or have a harvest or revival is as simple as the instructions Jesus gave to the seventy-two when he sent them:

Heal the sick who are there and tell them, "The Kingdom of God has come near to you."

LUKE 10:6-9

This model is the most effective, most scriptural model there is.

Those who Jesus sent—the apostles, the seventy-two, and all "those who believe"—were all trans-local ministers at the time. There was no church. They were sent out to begin a church, and to draw people to it. That is why the model is so important; it is the strategy Jesus gave for attracting crowds for the church.

If there are no signs and miracles through the power of the Spirit, are we really fully proclaiming the Gospel of Christ? There must be evidence of signs and wonders for the Gospel to be fully proclaimed. The Apostle Paul declared this:

> *Therefore I glory in Christ Jesus in my service to God. I will not venture to speak of anything except what Christ has accomplished through me in leading the Gentiles to obey God* **by what I have said and done—by the power of signs and miracles**, *through the power of the Spirit. So from Jerusalem all the way around to Illyricum,* **I have fully proclaimed the Gospel of Christ.**
>
> ROMANS 15:17-19 *(author emphasis)*

This model of ministry fulfilled the requirements of both Jew and Greek:

> *Jews demand signs and Greeks look for wisdom.*
>
> 1 CORINTHIANS 1:22

Jesus' words were the essence of wisdom, while giving the Jews what they demanded … signs.

A ministry to reach the Jews requires a strategy to show them signs. This is the approach the Scripture gives us for the Jew.

This is the order of ministry for the kind of success that occurred in the Gospels and with the early church. This model is for every ministry and for every Christian; it is the model Jesus gave us. We are all called to do the miraculous—things against natural law. We must do things which, to the natural eye and worldly understanding, do not make sense. By this we offer the best proof we have of the existence of the living God.

> MIRACLES OFFER THE BEST PROOF WE HAVE OF THE EXISTENCE OF THE LIVING GOD

Even before Jesus sent out those teams (twelve, seventy-two, and all who believe), it's interesting to note that the first person he sent out to minister was a restored demoniac, from the region of the Gardarenes (Mark 5:1-20).

Before his encounter with Jesus, the demoniac lived among the rocks and caves. He would break off the chains that bound him. He was kept under guard, and he didn't wear any clothes, but when he saw Jesus, he:

> *... cried out, and fell down before him and said with a loud voice, "What have you to do with me, Jesus, Son of the Most High God?"... And he begged Jesus again and again not to send them out of the area.*
>
> MARK 5:7 & 10

HE KILLED OUR PIGS

A large herd of pigs was feeding on the nearby hillside. The demons begged Jesus, "Send us among the pigs; allow us to go into them" (Mark 5:11-12). Jesus drove the demons out of the demoniac and the demons went into the pigs. The pigs rushed down an embankment into the lake and drowned.

Those tending the pigs ran off and reported this to the town and the people went out to see what had happened.

> *The whole town went out to meet Jesus. And when they saw him, they pleaded with him to leave their region.*
>
> MATTHEW 8:34

They met Jesus, but they never heard him preach or saw him heal the sick. Consequently, there was confusion as to who he was and what he did. They wanted him to leave the area, especially when they heard that a whole herd of pigs had been destroyed because of his words.

Through his encounter with Jesus, the demoniac was healed, saved, and sent out as a minister of the Gospel. God will use whomever is willing and available, and in the demoniac he found someone who fit those requirements. He told him to:

> *Go home to your own people and tell them how much the Lord has done for you, and how he has had mercy on you.*
>
> MARK 5:19

So the man went first to his family to tell them what the Lord had done for him, then he began telling those in the Decapolis (a ten-city area) of the Lord's mercy on him. We see the result of this man sharing his testimony of healing. He went to the Decapolis to prepare the ground for Jesus' visit there. In Matthew 15:29-31, we see the result of his ministry:

> *Jesus left there and went along the Sea of Galilee. Then he went up on a mountainside and sat down. Great crowds came to him, bringing the lame, the blind, the crippled, the mute, and many others, and laid them at his feet; and he healed them. The people were amazed when*

they saw the mute speaking, the crippled made well, the lame walking, and the blind seeing. And they praised the God of Israel.

The demoniac prepared the way for Jesus to visit the Decapolis. Although the demoniac didn't heal the sick, he was sent out with the same message of healing, of which he was the prime example.

Experience First

Some folks have never seen a miracle, so understandably they don't know what one looks like, feels like, sounds like, or how to respond after encountering one. If you have never seen a miracle, then your image of one is probably somewhat distorted. They look normal, sound normal, feel normal. In fact, most folks who have seen miracles say that they are normal in a supernatural way, because it is something that is supposed to happen. It's hard for someone who has never seen a miracle to believe for one, especially if they have been taught that they are not for today. With no basis for having faith for a miracle, most have a surrealistic, cosmic understanding of the miraculous.

In church meetings, many times I will tell the congregation that they are going to see some miracles, and that they are very simple occurrences. I also tell them they will see how simple miracles are brought about without raising one's voice. Often after someone has seen or experienced miracles, the response is, "Oh, that was so simple!" Once a person experiences a miracle, they then have a basis to believe for them, and their eyes will be opened to the Scriptures.

Many Christians do not believe in miracles. They know they are present in the Bible, but because they have never experienced one, they do not see them as valid for today. But if they witnessed miracles, they would have their eyes opened. It would change their theology because the Scriptures would then open to them.

When I first started praying for the sick and saw people get healed, I began to study the Word to validate what I saw happening. Some told me that miracles were for today, but until I started seeing them in my own life and ministry, I had never studied the subject of healing. I knew healing was in the Word, but knew very little about it until I started to do it. That is when the Holy Spirit opened my eyes to what the Scriptures say about healing.

The amount of Scripture the Holy Spirit devotes to healing is overwhelming; it was a major part of Jesus' ministry, and it should be an important part of every church's ministry. But it seems that we have to experience it first before we can see it in the Scriptures. This would explain why so many mainline churches don't have a clue that healing is for today.

Churches (and denominations) which have never experienced healing and miracles come to the conclusion that healing is a gift lost to the church. In reality, it is a loss of faith. They have excluded everything supernatural from their theology: healing, miracles, deliverance, tongues, ... things which require a level of faith beyond waiting around to go to Heaven.

Our natural senses are unreliable for discerning spiritual things. If we rely on our natural senses to discern spiritual things, we are destined to fail. That which is seen in the natural is unreliable. The Scriptures are the only source that is totally reliable:

> *Faith is being sure of what we hope for and certain of what we do not see.*
>
> HEBREWS 11:1

Secessionists believe these gifts have passed away. However, there is not one Scripture in the Bible which states that the gifts of healing and miracles have passed away. It takes only one miracle to prove that the age of miracles is not over.

We are a supernatural people from the new birth and on into eternity, including present day gifts and miracles. Our God is "the same yesterday, today, and forever." The Spirit-filled evangelical, charismatic, and Pentecostal churches are leading the way in growth and vitality around the world, while the others as a whole (mainline/denominational churches) are experiencing decline.

Apparently there are more than a few Southern Baptists who have experienced the supernatural. In *Christianity Today*, May 16, 1986, Pastor Don LeMaster of the West Lauderdale Baptist Church in Fort Lauderdale, Florida, estimated that 5% of SBC congregations were openly charismatic at that time. That number has probably increased since then. *Charisma* magazine, March 1999, contained a report entitled, "Shaking Southern Baptist Tradition," which gave many examples of charismatic Southern Baptist congregations. Once experienced, it is hard to dissuade those who have come into the experience. Once they have begun speaking in tongues, their eyes are opened to the Scriptures, and they are able to recognize the truth.

Miracles Can't Be Kept Secret

A miracle is:

- an extraordinary event manifesting divine intervention in human affairs, and

❧ an extremely outstanding or unusual event, thing, or accomplishment.[1]

It is difficult at best to distinguish between miracles of healing for a sickness of natural origin, and healing for a sickness caused by an evil spirit (which occurs when a demon is driven out of a person). Either way, both examples agree with Webster's definition of a miracle.

In Jesus' ministry, he didn't differentiate between a natural healing and a healing which occurs when a demon is driven out of someone. But in a conversation with the Apostle John, he did state that a miracle does occur when a demon is driven out:

> "Teacher," said John, "we saw someone driving out demons in your name and we told him to stop, because he was not one of us." "Do not stop him," Jesus said. "For no one who does a miracle in my name can in the next moment say anything bad about me."
>
> MARK 9:38-39

The wonderful thing about miracles is that they cannot be kept secret. There is an uncanny ability for news of a miracle to spread quickly. Jesus couldn't keep his miracles a secret, even though he tried. He healed a deaf man who was brought to him by friends and Jesus commanded them not to talk about it:

> Jesus commanded them not to tell anyone. But the more he did so, the more they kept talking about it. They did not obey Jesus; the people had no control when it came to obeying this command. The reason being, "People were overwhelmed with amazement."
>
> MARK 7:36-37

We could say that this was one failure of Jesus … but, of course, we say that in jest. It's comical that Jesus could not keep those who were healed from telling others. They would not obey that command. The reality is, a miracle can't be kept secret. People will want to talk about it, and others will want to hear about it. Miracles have an incredible ability to spread.

Jesus healed a man of leprosy and also gave him a strong warning not to tell anyone. I would think that if Jesus gave a strong warning to anyone, they would be fearful not to obey:

> *Jesus sent him away at once with a strong warning: "See that you don't tell this to anyone. But go, show yourself to the priest and offer the sacrifices that Moses commanded for your cleansing, as a testimony to them." Instead he went out and began to talk freely, spreading the news.*
>
> MARK 1:43-45

News of a miracle has the ability to reach all levels of society, as a member of the Sanhedrin admitted when they were trying to stop Peter and John from ministering in the name of Jesus:

> *"What are we going to do with these men?" they asked. "Everyone living in Jerusalem knows they have performed a notable sign, and we cannot deny it."*
>
> ACTS 4:16

Jesus' miracles and teachings are what set him apart from the kooks of the day like Theudas, who had about four-hundred followers, and Judas the Galilean, who led a band of people in revolt (Acts 5).

Jesus taught as one who had authority and not as the teachers of the law. What authenticated the message of the Kingdom were his miracles.

Even though Jesus instructed the people not to tell of his miracles, he expected them to believe him when they witnessed his miracles:

> *Then Jesus began to denounce the cities in which most of his miracles had been performed, because they did not repent. "Woe to you, Korazin! Woe to you, Bethsaida! If the miracles that were performed in you had been performed in Tyre and Sidon, they would have repented long ago in sackcloth and ashes."*
>
> MATTHEW 11:20-21

He clearly states that his miracles were proof of who he was, and if some didn't believe, it was to their own destruction. It's strong language that Jesus used; he denounced those cities (Chorazin, Bethsaida, and Capernaum) for their refusal to believe.

In John 14:11, Jesus said, "Believe me when I say that I am in the Father and the Father is in me; or at least believe on the evidence of the miracles themselves." Once again, miracles were an evidence for who Jesus was, and it is that evidence that authenticates the Gospel.

Healing and miracles have the same effect on people today as they did during the time of the early church. It will even cause agnostics and atheists to give pause to their unbelief, if not to totally believe in Jesus as Savior.

God testified about salvation by using signs, wonders, and miracles:

> *How shall we escape if we ignore so great a salvation? This salvation, which was first announced by the Lord, was confirmed to us by those who heard him. God also testified to it by signs, wonders, and various miracles, and by gifts of the Holy Spirit distributed according to his will.*

HEBREWS 2:3-4

A friend of mine invited me to speak to a group of unbelievers, but I didn't realize the group was so openly hostile to the Gospel until I got to the meeting. I started out by giving a simple message, and when I got through, their questions were outrageous. They blamed God for everything: Why does God allow babies to die? Why does God allow wars to go on? Why does God allow poverty and hunger? I didn't say anything, but there were Christians present to answer their questions. After about twenty minutes when things had settled down a little, I asked a very simple question: "Who would like to see a demonstration of God's power?" They all looked at me puzzled, but they all agreed that they wanted to see a demonstration of God's power. I wanted to stretch my faith, and this was a great opportunity.

I asked for anyone who had any illness to come up, and a girl in her twenties came forward. She had a great deal of pain throughout her entire body. As I spoke a word over her the Lord touched her, and she was totally healed, and began to cry softly. It was a touching scene as she stood in the center of the room telling how for the first time in many years she was pain-free. Others came forward and were healed. Now the group was stone silent. The people, who moments before were reluctant listeners, were all of a sudden quiet and sitting on the edge of their chairs, wanting to hear more. They were now willing to listen because of what they had witnessed. Before the meeting was over, they all received the Lord as Savior. They all knew the Gospel was real because of the

> THEY WERE NOW WILLING TO LISTEN BECAUSE OF WHAT THEY HAD WITNESSED

demonstration of God's power in their midst, which any Spirit-filled Christian can demonstrate.

As you will see, healing the sick is not just for a few gifted people to do. It is simple, and any Christian can do it, and do it effectively. It only takes a little faith, which every Christian has, or you wouldn't be a Christian.

The Scriptures say that it's a simple thing, but we filter the Scriptures through our insecurities, fears, and circumstances. Consequently, we get a worldly understanding, rather than biblical power, which comes through faith.

Paul speaks of the importance of ministering in the power of God in 1 Corinthians 2:1-5:

> *When I came to you, brothers, I did not come with eloquence or superior wisdom as I proclaimed to you the testimony about God. For I resolved to know nothing while I was with you except Jesus Christ and Him crucified. I came to you in weakness and fear, and with much trembling. My message and my preaching were not with wise and persuasive words, but with a demonstration of the Spirit's power, so that your faith might not rest on men's wisdom, but on God's power.*

Many preachers can demonstrate the power of God in their preaching and teaching, but without a demonstration of the Holy Spirit's power in signs, wonders, and miracles. Some preaching can be natural ability, but natural ability is not the issue. The issue is what the Spirit of God can do through us.

All born-again, Spirit-filled Christians have the same Holy Spirit power as the apostle Paul. Faith is the issue. It is faith that releases the power.

When we authenticate the Gospel, no one will have an answer for what they saw and heard—they can only say that it was God.

SHOW AND TELL

The heathen says there is no proof of God, however, the proof of God's existence is signs, wonders, and miracles; they validate the Gospel! As Jesus said to the royal official whose son was close to death:

> *"Unless you people see miraculous signs and wonders," Jesus told him, "you will never believe."*
>
> JOHN 4:48

Miracles have the ability to give flesh and bones to the Gospel message. There is a merging of the Gospel message and the miraculous.

Unlike all the other religions of the world, Christianity has real power—the power of the Holy Spirit. And although the Kingdom may have multiplied millions (or trillions) of messages and teachings, it is the signs, wonders, and miracles, along with the Kingdom message, that will eliminate doubt and cause multitudes to believe. Signs, wonders, and miracles point to God, as when the early disciples went and preached everywhere:

SIGNS, WONDERS, AND MIRACLES POINT TO GOD

> *The Lord worked with them and confirmed his word by the signs that accompanied it.*
>
> MARK 16:20

John the Baptist was called by the Father to introduce Jesus to the world, but when he was imprisoned by Herod, he had doubt about Jesus' identity and wanted an answer. John's whole life was devoted to this calling. The Scripture says this about John:

> *This is he who was spoken of through the prophet Isaiah: A voice of one calling in the desert, "Prepare the way for the Lord, make straight paths for him."*
>
> MATTHEW 3:3

John was sure of many things in his life: his calling, his message, and to whom his message was for. However, there came a time when in prison, that he began to have doubt as to the positive identity of the Messiah, Jesus.

When King Herod put John the Baptist in prison, John desperately wanted to make sure that Jesus was the Messiah and not a fraud, or another forerunner like John himself. While spending time in that dark, damp, prison, John probably had some understanding that he was in deep trouble as a prisoner of Herod, and something bad could happen.

He had to have the answer to this burning question: Is Jesus the Messiah?

However, John the Baptist did know Jesus; he had baptized Jesus in the Jordan river, and recognized him as the Messiah. This is what John said when he first saw Jesus coming toward him:

> *Look, the Lamb of God, who takes away the sin of the world! This is the one I meant when I said, "A man who comes after me has surpassed me because he was before me."I myself did not know him, but the reason I came baptizing with water was that he might be revealed to Israel.*
>
> JOHN 1:30-31

John also gave this testimony about Jesus:

I saw the Spirit come down from Heaven as a dove and remain on him. And I myself did not know him, but the one who sent me to baptize with water told me, "The man on whom you see the Spirit come down and remain is the one who will baptize with the Holy Spirit." I have seen and I testify that this is God's Chosen One.

JOHN 1:32-34

John the Baptist should not have had any doubt about who Jesus was. However, in Herod's prison, John was having doubt and wanted to make sure he had not made a mistake. So, John sent his disciples to ask Jesus:

"Are you the one who was to come, or should we expect someone else?"

LUKE 7:20

Jesus gave a simple answer:

"The blind receive sight, the lame walk, those who have leprosy are cured. Go back and report to John what you have seen and heard: the deaf hear, the dead are raised, and the good news is preached to the poor."

LUKE 7:22

Jesus was saying that the only things necessary to validate him as being the Messiah were his preaching/teaching, and miracles of healing. It was not one or the other; it was both.

John had doubt about Jesus as the Messiah because he had never heard him preach or seen him heal the sick, but when John's disciples reported to him what they had seen and heard (preaching and healing), he then was satisfied that Jesus was the Messiah.

Because of the miracles, most people accepted that Jesus came from God. When Jesus healed a man born blind (John 9:1-34), the man was questioned by the Pharisees, who wanted to find some way to condemn Jesus. But the blind man had it right; he told the Pharisees:

> *"Nobody has ever heard of opening the eyes of a man born blind. If this man were not from God, he could do nothing."*
>
> JOHN 9:32-33

The blind man was correct. The proof that Jesus was from God was the fact that he could open the eyes of someone born blind. It validated that he truly came from God.

THE GREATEST MIRACLE

I once heard it said that a miracle is defined by how many times we've seen it. According to that understanding, if we see a certain miracle frequently, it becomes commonplace. I don't hold to that understanding of a miracle, but it gives us some understanding why some would take their salvation for granted. Salvation is still the greatest miracle of all. The resurrection of Jesus would be meaningless unless we were saved from sin. It would be, perhaps, an interesting story, but nothing more if the blood of the Lamb did not save us. There is no doubt that the greatest miracle is the fact that we can be saved from sin and go to Heaven to live with God.

If we then can believe the greatest miracle in all of history, why do some have a tough time believing in signs, wonders, and miracles of healing? The greatest miracle in our life has already occurred. The greatest miracle in the Bible is not the parting of the Red Sea or Jonah in the belly of a fish, or even the resurrection. For the Christian, the greatest miracle is the fact that we are saved and will go to Heaven. So, if we believe that we are saved and going to Heaven, it should be easy to believe in signs, wonders, and miracles. A miracle of healing is a very simple, elementary thing compared to salvation.

I prayed with a life-long friend of mine to be born again, and as he was sitting there trying to hide the tears rolling down his cheeks, I asked him if I could pray for his healing. He replied, "I don't believe in miracles." So I didn't go against his wishes. He didn't believe in miracles, and yet the greatest miracle in his life had just occurred.

> COMPARED TO SALVATION, A MIRACLE OF HEALING IS A SIMPLE THING

We have no trouble believing that vitamins really work, or that the sun is coming up in the morning, or a light bulb is going to light up when we flip a switch, so we shouldn't have any trouble believing that if we lay hands on a sick person, that they will recover.

The last several years of my father's life, he was in poor health, suffering from several serious ailments. Mom called one day and said that dad was in the hospital and it was doubtful whether he would make it through the night. I drove the twelve hours from Birmingham, Alabama to Irving, Texas where my parents lived. When I got there I went to the hospital. When I approached dad's hospital room I could hear him talking to someone and it sounded like he was in a really good mood. When I walked in the room I knew something was dramatically different. Dad said to me, "Buster (that's my family nickname), you won't believe what happened to me last night." He began telling the most incredible story; he said, "The Lord took me to Heaven last night. It is the most beautiful place imaginable, and the way that you feel when you are there can't be described. I didn't see the Lord, but he kept saying, 'That's right; just follow me.'"

My father could not wait to die. He said, "The Lord told me that I wasn't going to die now, but I was going to die soon."

He told my mother, "Molly, why don't you die with me?"

She said, "No, I think I'll wait a while."

He also wanted my sisters and brother to die with him, but "You," he told me, "you have to stay." Because I led him to the Lord, he wanted me to remain and continue in the ministry. My dad was really excited about dying because he had seen the reality of Heaven … and he knew it was the greatest miracle of all.

ENDNOTE

1. "Miracle." *Merriam-Webster's Collegiate Dictionary Tenth Edition.* 10th ed. 1994. Print.

Chapter Two

Give It Away

In January 2007, I had a dream. When I awoke, I knew God had spoken to me, but I wasn't exactly sure what he was trying to convey.

In the dream, I was in some kind of a religious meeting. I was sitting with friends in the back of the auditorium, which appeared to seat around 400-500 people. A man approached me from behind and said, "You don't belong here. You don't have a collar on," pointing to my neck where a clergy collar would be. I didn't recognize the man, but I said to him, "I don't wear a collar, and furthermore, I don't need one." The man appeared angry, and walked off in a huff. When I turned around to face the front of the auditorium, the large group of people sitting in front of me had divided into two groups with Muslims on the left and Catholics (who were unsaved) on the right. At that moment the Lord spoke to me and said, "They will believe when they see miracles."

I knew that the Lord was trying to tell me something, but how could such a multitude of people see the miracles necessary for them to believe in the living God?

I sought the Lord for an answer to the dream for several days, and one day while in prayer the Lord said to me, "Give your gift away." My first reaction to giving (imparting) the gift of healing to others was carnal. "If I do that," I thought, "I won't have a ministry!" However, it didn't take long for me to realize that that was exactly what I wanted—others healing the sick and doing miracles for all to see. This was clearly God's strategy for the Gospel to be made real to the unbeliever.

Giving the gift away was what God wanted me to do so I began imparting the healing gift to others. During one church service I called up a twelve-year-old boy and coached him as he prayed for the sick. Everyone he prayed for was healed. On dozens of other occasions I had seen the gift imparted with incredible results. Healing is not rocket science; it's a promise of God. It is definitely a simple thing to do for everyone in the Body of Christ.

The Impartation of Spiritual Gifts

Simon the Sorcerer amazed the people of Samaria with his sorcery. They said of him that he was the divine power known as the Great Power, and they followed him because he had astounded them for a long time with his magic:

> *When Simon saw that the Spirit was given at the laying on of the apostles' hands, he offered them money and said, "Give me also this ability so that everyone on whom I lay my hands may receive the Holy Spirit."*
>
> ACTS 8:18-19

Likely he thought that if he could impart the Holy Spirit to folks, he could continue to amaze them with his magic. He had it all wrong of course, and had to be rebuked by Peter. The impartation of the Holy Spirit is to glorify Jesus, not some magic trick to glorify man.

Some might be offended by the term "impartation," preferring instead to use the word "release" (of the gifts). Whichever term you favor is not a problem. Call it what you like, it's the same thing and it is scriptural. Paul, in anticipation of visiting the Roman Christians, said this:

> *"I long to see you so that I may impart to you some spiritual gift to make you strong."*
>
> ROMANS 1:11

Paul eagerly anticipated meeting with the Roman Christians. The thing he wanted to do for them was to impart some spiritual gift, and the result would make them strong. Strong for what purpose? So they could and would carry out the purpose of God that was in them. Every Christian has a destiny, purpose, and an assignment (or assignments) in God, and the impartation of a spiritual gift strengthens us to carry out that purpose.

The impartation of spiritual gifts is an apostolic gift, used to equip the saints. Moses is an Old Testament type of apostle who imparted the gift of wisdom to Joshua:

> *Now Joshua son of Nun was filled with the spirit of wisdom because Moses had laid his hands on him. So the Israelites listened to him and did what the Lord had commanded Moses.*
>
> DEUTERONOMY 34:9

Moses equipped Joshua to take over the leadership of Israel and lead them across the Jordan into the Promised Land by laying hands on him and filling him with the spirit of wisdom.

The Apostle Paul imparted a spiritual gift to Timothy:

"For this reason I remind you to fan into flame the gift of God, which is in you through the laying on of my hands. For God did not give us a spirit of timidity, but a spirit of power, of love and of self-discipline."

2 TIMOTHY 1:6-7

Because of Timothy's timid nature, he needed some encouragement to use his gift, so Paul encouraged him to do so. He told Timothy to "fan into flame" the gift he had been given—the same way we fan into flame any gift, by simply using it boldly and in faith. Spiritual gifts are usually given in an embryonic stage—an ember that when fanned will become a flame. When we use a spiritual gift, it will stretch our faith. We use spiritual gifts according to our faith. If your faith is not strong, even though you have a spiritual gift, you may be hesitant to use it.

When Paul was in Ephesus, he told the people that John's baptism had been a baptism of repentence and that they should believe in the one coming after John—Jesus.

On hearing this, they were baptized in the name of the Lord Jesus. When Paul placed his hands on them, the Holy Spirit came on them, and they spoke in tongues and prophesied. There were about twelve men in all.

ACTS 19:4-7

After Paul was struck blind on the way to Damascus, Ananais equipped him when he laid hands on him to restore his sight and fill him with the Holy Spirit:

> *Then Ananias went to the house and entered it. Placing his hands on Saul, he said, "Brother Saul, the Lord Jesus, who appeared to you on the road as you were coming here has sent me so that you may see again and be filled with the Holy Spirit."*
>
> ACTS 9:17

Notice that Ananais laid hands on Paul not only to restore his sight, but also to fill him with the Holy Spirit. Paul was strengthened by the healing and then filled with the Holy Spirit to carry out his purpose in God.

Jesus imparted power and authority to the apostles in Luke 9:1, and to the seventy-two in Luke 10:19. He did so to send them to <u>proclaim the Kingdom</u> and <u>heal the sick</u>.

Jesus also gave the command to another group, saying:

> *"These signs will accompany those who believe ... they will place their hands on sick people, and they will get well."*
>
> MARK 16:17 & 18

The widening circle went from the twelve, to the seventy-two, then to every Christian who exhibits faith ("those who believe").

Jesus sent the first two groups with power and authority with no conditions attached, but the larger group of all Christians, he sent with the condition that they exhibit faith.

He didn't send the twelve apostles or the seventy-two by saying, "This is for all who believe." They didn't need to be told that they had to have faith; they had faith; they had been with Jesus, and were personally taught by him. They knew Jesus intimately.

The groups of twelve and seventy-two were given the Holy Spirit before the day of Pentecost for the purpose of casting out demons and healing the sick. The power that was given can only be interpreted one way and that is the Holy Spirit:

> *Jesus had called the twelve together, he gave them power and authority to drive out all demons and to cure diseases, and he sent them out to proclaim the kingdom of God and to heal the sick.*
>
> LUKE 9:1-2

SPIRITUAL GIFTS REQUIRE FAITH FOR THEIR OPERATION

Even though spiritual gifts are imparted, it still requires faith for their operation. We are all given the same amount of power because we are all given the same Holy Spirit (as given on the day of Pentecost), but to release the power of the Holy Spirit requires faith.

Spiritual gifts are given to build up the believer, to make them strong, as in the case of Christians in the New Testament and Joshua in the Old Testament.

GIFTS ARE GIVEN

God's gifts are not given on a reward system. They are not given according to works, for accomplishments, or maturity; nor is giftedness a sign of maturity. This is obvious when we see gifted Christians who are carnal.

You don't have to be super spiritual to receive spiritual gifts (although it might help). The Apostle Paul is a good example, he was not super spiritual when he received the gift of the Holy Spirit. He was on his way to persecute Christians when he was struck down on the Road to Damascus:

> *Saul was still breathing out murderous threats against the Lord's disciples. He went to the high priest and asked him for letters to the synagogues in Damascus, so that if he found any there who belonged to the Way, whether men or women, he might take them as prisoners to Jerusalem.*
>
> ACTS 9:1-2

I have known some people who were mature Christians and very spiritual who could not receive the gift of tongues (a simple gift to receive). They were not able to receive the gift simply, as a child. Instead they would over-analyze and spiritualize it, making it complicated and too difficult to grasp. Receiving the gift of healing seems to cross all barriers and is easily imparted to everyone. However, if someone really wants to become proficient, the gift must be fanned into a flame.

Joseph fanned into flame his gift of administration. Put another way, God provoked Joseph to fan into flame his gift of administration when he was sold into slavery by his brothers. Joseph was bought by Potiphar, who was one of Pharaoh's officials, the captain of the guard, and was put in charge of all the household duties. Joseph had no choice and became the administrator of Potiphar's house.

From Potiphar's house, he was put in jail because of bogus charges brought against him by Potiphar's wife. While in jail, he was put in charge of "all those held in the prison, and he was made responsible for all that was done there" (Genesis 39:22).

Joseph went from administering one household to administering a prison, and this is what prepared him to become the administrator for a country—Egypt. Pharaoh put him in charge of the whole land of Egypt. God brought Joseph through the necessary stages which caused his gift of administration to be fanned into flame in order to be totally proficient to administer all of Egypt. All gifts need to be used, exercised, and fanned. This is how we become proficient using them.

In 1 Corinthians 12:11, it says that the gifts are given to each one just as he determines. God desires to give us spiritual gifts, and there are only simple requirements for the Christian to receive spiritual gifts:

There must be a desire to have the gifts. We are instructed to:

Eagerly desire the greater gifts.

1 CORINTHIANS 12:31

Also, if you want spiritual gifts, You must ask for them:

Which of you fathers, if your son asks for a fish, will give him a snake instead? Or if he asks for an egg, will give him a scorpion? If you then, though you are evil, know how to give good gifts to your children, how much more will your Father in Heaven give the Holy Spirit to those who ask him?

LUKE 11:11).

If you ask God, he will give you the gifts that you desire. Of course, the gifts are distributed according to the determination of the Holy Spirit (1 Corinthians 12:11), but if there is a desire on your part, it is likely that you can have that particular gift.

A person must want the gifts and ask for the gifts. I was debating whether to add a third requirement (faith), but my experience has taught me that it only takes a small amount of faith, which every Christian has. It says in Matthew 17:20-21, that with just a small amount of faith, we can move a mountain. However, I must clarify a key point. Faith is an important component of the healing ministry, and with a small amount of faith it is relatively easy to heal the sick in a Christian setting, among believers. But a higher degree of faith is required when an individual is healing people among non-believers and skeptics.

It helps if a person is a mature Christian and full of faith, but from my experience it is not always necessary to have bold faith. Let me give some examples of what I mean:

I was in a church in Ohio, and I asked the pastor to choose some folks from his congregation who he would like to see get the impartation of the gift of healing. When we called those individuals up to receive the impartation they balked, made excuses, and reluctantly came forward. I imparted the gift of healing and coached them and had them heal at least two people each. They may never heal anyone ever again, but in that instance, they all did.

I asked the pastor at lunch about the folks that he chose, and he told me that he chose people that were immature and/or came to church only on occasion.

In another church in upstate New York, before the service began, I was walking up from the basement of the church where the youth group had just been released from a prayer meeting, and I overheard a young girl behind me say excitedly, "That was my first Pentecostal prayer meeting."

I turned to her and asked if she had ever prayed for someone's healing? She said, "No." I then asked her if she would like to have the gift of healing, but she had no idea what I was talking about. I told her that I would be ministering in the service, and that she would be a perfect candidate. I called her forward after my message and imparted the gift to her, and she (through the Lord) healed two people with serious illnesses.

I know many examples of Christians who, although they were not mature believers, could immediately begin healing the sick. I do want to mention one other example: a Baptist pastor (a mature man of God) who attended a meeting where I was ministering. When I imparted the gift to him, he began healing folks with tears streaming down his face. He realized for the first time that healing was for today.

DUBIOUS CHARACTERS

In Scripture we see a number of dubious characters who performed signs, wonders, and miracles. Some of them are totally false and their miracles are only counterfeit. However, there are others who are able to perform miracles even though they didn't have a relationship with Jesus.

1. *"The coming of the lawless one will be in accordance with the work of Satan displayed in all kinds of counterfeit miracles, signs, and wonders."*

    2 THESSALONIANS 2:9

    - Satan knows that if he is to be like God, he has to perform miracles, signs, and wonders … but he can produce only counterfeits.

2. *"False christs and false prophets will appear and perform signs and miracles to deceive the elect—if that were possible."*

    MARK 13:22

    - False christs and false prophets are a class of people that have fallen away from God, but can still perform signs and miracles. Faith can still operate because God's gifts and calling are irrevocable (Romans 11:29), but they operate for their selfish glorification, and not for God.

3. *"Not everyone who says to me, 'Lord, Lord,' will enter the Kingdom of Heaven, but only the one who does the will of my Father who is in Heaven. Many will say to me on that day, 'Lord, Lord, did we not prophesy in your name and in your name drive out demons and in your name perform many miracles?' Then I will tell them plainly, 'I never knew you. Away from me, you evildoers!'"*

   MATTHEW 7:21.

   - Although this group can perform miracles, Jesus describes them as "evildoers." So obviously, doing miracles doesn't necessarily mean you have a relationship with Jesus, for Jesus said to this group (of many), "I never knew you. Away from me, you evildoers!" This group (many) were at one time Christian, but even though they had forsaken Jesus, they could still do miracles.

4. *"If I have the gift of prophecy and can fathom all mysteries and all knowledge, and if I have a faith that can move mountains, but do not have love, I am nothing."*

   1 CORINTHIANS 13:2

   - Mountain-moving faith, operating independently of love, has no value to the person doing it. It could bless someone else by healing them, but is meaningless for the person doing it, when done without love. Again we see that miracles can be performed without being fully committed to Christ, but that ministry ends in tragedy.

5. Judas had charge of the moneybag and used to help himself to what was in it (John 12:6), and later betrayed Jesus for thirty pieces of silver. Judas was chosen as an apostle sent out to do the work of the ministry, and he was among those who Jesus sent to the places where he was going to visit.

6. *One of the disciples said to Jesus, "We saw someone driving out demons in your name and we told him to stop, because he was not one of us. 'Do not stop him,' Jesus said. 'For no one who does a miracle in my name can in the next moment say anything bad about me, for whoever is not against us is for us.'"*

MARK 9:38-40

- The disciples saw a man driving out demons who they didn't recognize. He was probably someone that viewed the ministry of Jesus from afar and thought he would try healing the sick; behold, it worked!

7. *"Some Jews who went around driving out evil spirits tried to invoke the name of the Lord Jesus over those who were demon-possessed. They would say, 'In the name of the Jesus whom Paul preaches, I command you to come out.'"*

ACTS 19:13

- These Jews were not disciples. They were seven sons of a Jewish chief priest who were actually driving out evil spirits in the name of Jesus. They had probably witnessed this occurring among the disciples, so they started doing it with some success until they tried to drive out a demon that overpowered them, and they ran off naked and bleeding.

8. *"The seventy-two returned with joy and said, 'Lord, even the demons submit to us in your name.'"*

LUKE 10:17

- They were all novices and were surprised when they experienced demons submitting to their authority. It was the first time they had dealt with demons, although they had seen Jesus do it, and possibly saw the apostles doing it.

There is a wide range of people performing signs, wonders, and miracles, including Satan (with counterfeit miracles), false christs, false prophets, and mountain movers. Jesus would not be working with any of them in healing and miracles, but he does work with Christians (Mark 16:20).

At the other extreme, we see the apostles—Peter, Paul, and others—who went on to a "greater things" ministry in terms of healing and miracles. They raised the dead, healed cripples, set free the demonized, etc. Miracles will happen because we believe what we've heard from the Scriptures:

> *Does God give you his Spirit and work miracles among you by the works of the law, or by your believing what you heard?*
>
> GALATIANS 3:5

The Apostle Paul is contrasting the works of the law versus believing the Gospel, and the conclusion is that miracles happen when we simply have faith.

It is significant that if those false and dubious characters can heal the sick and perform miracles, then the average Christian can certainly heal the sick, raise the dead, cleanse the leper, and drive out demons.

GIFTS OF HEALING

It says in 1 Corinthians 12:9, that there are "gifts of healing." The word *gifts* is plural, which means that there are diverse gifts of healing. In other words, there could be a gift for healing eyes, another for ears, and another for arthritis, cancer, migraines, etc., or you may have several of the various gifts, and can heal many types of sicknesses and diseases.

The question I have about the gift of healing is, what is it comprised of? Is the gift of healing separate from the three components of healing: faith, power, or authority? Since, faith, power, and authority are the three components of healing, the gift of healing must have one or all three of these components.

When Jesus sent out the apostles (Luke 9:1) and the seventy-two (Luke 10:1) for the first time, he gave them authority. Why didn't he give them the gift of healing? The likely answer is that the gift of healing is authority.

We are all given the same Holy Spirit, therefore, we all have the same amount of power. We are given a measure of faith and any faith beyond that comes through the testing of our faith. One of the three components which is given differently is authority.

When Jesus sent out the apostles for the first time to go to the towns where he was going, he gave them power and authority. Jesus gave them power because they had not yet been baptized in the Holy Spirt and they needed the power.

> THE GIFT OF HEALING AND AUTHORITY ARE ONE AND THE SAME

The second group Jesus sent out was the seventy-two. When he sent them, he only gave them authority (Luke 10:19). I'm assuming that they already had power because there is no mention of them being given power for the task. From this reasoning, at this point, I believe that the gift of healing and authority are one and the same. It is clear from scripture that it is a word (or words) of authority that we use to heal the sick and drive out demons.

3
CHAPTER THREE

IT'S ALL GOD

It all begins with the name of Jesus: salvation, signs, wonders, miracles, etc. It is the name of Jesus we can trust when performing signs, wonders, and miracles. In our relationship with Jesus, he gives us permission to use his name against all ungodliness. There is awesome power in that name, and it is the name of Jesus that is above every name in heaven, on earth, or under the earth.

> *Therefore God exalted him to the highest place and gave him the name that is above every name, that at the name of Jesus every knee should bow, in heaven and on earth and under the earth and every tongue acknowledge that Jesus Christ is Lord, to the glory of God the Father.*
>
> PHILIPPIANS 2:9-11

I hate it when I hear people use the Lord's name, "Jesus Christ," as a curse word, but I also find it interesting that they use his name at all. Why don't people who want to curse say, Buddha or Mohammed or Baal or Satan? It is because those names don't have any power or significance, but the name of Jesus has a reality even if the person using it as a curse word doesn't know it. If you are speaking to a non-Christian and the name Jesus is mentioned, there is a reaction even if it isn't obvious, but if the name Buddha or Mohammed or Baal or Satan is mentioned, there is no reaction because those names have no power or relevance. It is only the name of Jesus that has real power, and is to be exalted above every other name.

We have permission to use the name of Jesus and the authority that goes with it. In that name there is power and authority, and when we say, "in the name of Jesus be healed," people will be healed, demons will flee, and signs, wonders, and miracles will occur because of the power in that name.

It preempts all other names, thrones, personalities, devils, etc., and it demands a response because it is the supreme name in all the earth, and with permission to use his name comes access to his power and authority:

> *The Son is the image of the invisible God, the firstborn over all creation. For in him all things were created: things in heaven and on earth, visible and invisible, whether thrones or powers or rulers or authorities; all things have been created through him and for him. He is before all things, and in him all things hold together. And he is the head of the body, the church; he is the beginning and the firstborn from among the dead, so that in everything he might have the supremacy. For God was pleased to have all his fullness dwell in him.*
>
> COLOSSIANS 1:15-19

Peter demonstrated the power in the name of Jesus in his encounter with a crippled beggar. After Peter healed the beggar at the gate beautiful, he offered this explanation to an astonished crowd:

"You disowned the Holy and Righteous One and asked that a murderer be released to you. You killed the author of life, but God raised him from the dead. We are witnesses of this. By faith in the name of Jesus, this man whom you see and know was made strong. It is Jesus' name and the faith that comes through him that has completely healed him, as you can all see."

ACTS 3:14-16

What Peter said could be paraphrased in this way: "Jesus said that we could use his name, so I did, and power was released and the crippled man was healed."

I saw some video footage from a surveillance camera of a man robbing a jewelry store, and the lady who owned the store confronted the robber and said, "Get out of my store in Jesus' name." She repeated it several times until the robber turned around with gun in hand and left the store. The lady later said that the man appeared stunned and confused, like there was a barrier in front of him, which he couldn't cross.

A friend of mine who did a lot of cycling would ride in a section of road where there were a lot of dogs running loose. I asked him one day how he was able to ride through that section without getting bitten. He told me that they would start to chase him as he peddled up the hill, but as soon as he would yell, "In Jesus' name leave," they would retreat. Things like that happen because the name of Jesus carries power and authority. That's why Peter's shadow healed people as he walked by.

In healing the sick or casting out a demon, the emphasis is on the name of Jesus because of its power. Jesus said:

"In my name they will drive out demons; they will speak in new tongues; they will pick up snakes with their hands; and when they

drink deadly poison, it will not hurt them at all; they will place their hands on sick people, and they will get well."

MARK 16:17-18

Some Jews who went around driving out evil spirits tried to invoke the name of Jesus over those who were demon-possessed. They would say, "In the name of Jesus, whom Paul preaches, I command you to come out" (Acts 19:13-6). Yet all seven of the men were overpowered and beaten up by the demon they were trying to drive out. They were forced to run out of the house naked and bleeding. They attempted to use the name of Jesus, but because they didn't know Jesus, they didn't have the permission to use his name—Christians do!

The demons know about your relationship with Jesus. They make it their business to know things like that. Are you saved? Are you Spirit-filled? Then you have every right to use that name; in fact, Jesus wants you to use his name. He gave you permission to use it.

> DEMONS KNOW ABOUT YOUR RELATIONSHIP WITH JESUS

We have permission to use the name of Jesus, but it still takes faith to release the Holy Ghost power within. Does one Christian have more power than another? No! We have the same power but different levels of faith which release the power.

Stephen was chosen to be a deacon in the early church, and Acts 6:5 says this about him:

They chose Stephen, a man full of faith and of the Holy Spirit, and because of his faith, he performed great wonders and signs among the people.

ACTS 6:8

He was not an apostle or prophet, but a deacon, yet he did great signs and wonders because of his faith.

It may take a few confrontations with demons before they know who you are, but they will know who you are shortly. We are protected by the power of his name (John 17:11). This protection is for all Christians all the time, and under all circumstances. Keep in mind what Jesus said about being protected from the enemy:

> *I have given you authority to trample on snakes and scorpions and to overcome all the power of the enemy; nothing will harm you.*
>
> LUKE 10:19

Three Components

There are three passive components to healing, they are:

- faith,
- power,
- and authority.

I call them passive because they remain neutral until they are initiated by using the name of Jesus, or laying on of hands, or speaking to the mountain. As we take a close look at these passive components we see that it is the totality of God. It is Jesus, the Holy Spirit, and the Father who are the three components of healing: faith, power, and authority.

1. **Faith:** It is faith in Jesus that opens the way to a relationship with the Father and releases the power of the Holy Spirit. It is faith in Jesus that tells us that we can heal the sick:

> *If you have faith as small as a mustard seed, you can say to this mountain, "Move from here to there," and it will move. Nothing will be impossible for you.*
>
> MATTHEW 17:20

2. Power: The baptism in the Holy Spirit was given on the day of Pentecost for the purpose of receiving power to be a witness:

> *You will receive power when the Holy Spirit comes on you; and you will be my witnesses in Jerusalem, and in all Judea and Samaria, and to the ends of the earth.*
>
> ACTS 1:8

3. Authority: All authority is derived from the Father:

> *I have given you authority to trample on snakes and scorpions and to overcome all the power of the enemy.*
>
> LUKE 10:19

> *For as the Father has life in himself, so he has granted the Son also to have life in himself. And he has given him authority to judge because he is the Son of Man.*
>
> JOHN 5:26-27

It is always faith, power, and authority working together to bring about signs, wonders, and miracles of healing. The three work together as in the following Scripture when Jesus sent out the twelve apostles for the first time:

> *When [1] Jesus had called the Twelve together, he gave them [2] power, and [3] authority to drive out all demons and to cure diseases."*
>
> LUKE 9:1 (numbers added)

When a healing occurs, it is the triune God who is involved in it. God is not a neutral observer, but is totally involved in the outcome.

Three Aggressive Components of Healing

There are also three aggressive components of healing, which are:

- permission to use the name Jesus,
- speaking to the sickness/demon,
- and laying on of hands.

Just like the the three passive components of healing, the three aggressive components are also the totality of God:

1. **The name of Jesus:** Jesus says that we can use his name, and in that name, there is access to the Father (authority) and to the Holy Spirit (power):

    > *By faith in the name of Jesus, this man whom you see and know was made strong. It is Jesus' name and the faith that comes through him that has completely healed him, as you can all see.*
    >
    > ACTS 3:16

    > *I will do whatever you ask in my name, so that the Father may be glorified in the Son. You may ask me for anything in my name, and I will do it.*
    >
    > JOHN 14:13-14

2. Speaking to the mountain: Jesus said that we can speak to the mountain and it will be removed. We are to speak directly to the issue, whether it's a need for healing or deliverance. In Genesis 1, God created the heavens and the earth, and he did so by speaking things into existence. And to a limited degree he has given us creative ability to remove certain issues that pertain to healing and deliverance.

> *Then the disciples came to Jesus in private and asked, "Why couldn't we drive it out?" He replied, "Because you have so little faith. Truly I tell you, if you have faith as small as a mustard seed, you can say to this mountain, 'Move from here to there,' and it will move. Nothing will be impossible for you."*
>
> MATTHEW 17:19-20

3. The laying on of hands:

> *They will place their hands on sick people, and they will get well.*
>
> MARK 16:18

In the following verse we see the three methods working together, but that isn't always the case. Speaking to the problem and laying on of hands can be done separate from one another. However, in the following verse they are all working together:

> *Jesus [1] reached out his hand and [2] touched the man. "I am willing," he said. "Be clean!" [3] Immediately he was cleansed of his leprosy.*
>
> MATTHEW 8:3 *(numbers added)*

In the case of the three passive components of healing (faith, power, and authority), and the three aggressive components of healing (Jesus' name, speaking, and laying on hands), God is not a neutral observer, but is totally involved when a healing occurs.

Two of the aggressive components—laying hands on the sick person or speaking to the illness—are optional. We can lay hands on the sick or we can speak to the situation; we don't always have to do both. There are situations where we can't lay hands on the person. They could be possibly be in another location or we could be on the telephone with them. Consequently, we have the option of either speaking to the situation or laying hands on the person. However, if the person were present, it would be better to do both.

Jesus Will Work With Us

It is obvious that Jesus will work with us in healing the sick because the healing process is all about him. He worked with the early disciples to assure that they had success:

> *After the Lord Jesus had spoken to them, he was taken up into heaven and he sat at the right hand of God. Then the disciples went out and preached everywhere, and the Lord worked with them and confirmed his word by the signs that accompanied it.*
>
> MARK 16:19-20

Signs, wonders, and miracles originate in the heart of God, in the very depths of who he is; his desire is to see them carried out on earth. Jesus said this about the origination of signs, wonders, and miracles:

> *Do not believe me unless I do the works of my Father. But if I do them, even though you do not believe me, believe the works, that you may know and understand that the Father is in me, and I in the Father.*
>
> JOHN 10:37-38

We are simply jars of clay (2 Corinthians 4:7) who God is willing to display His all-surpassing power through, and he will literally work with us to do so. Our part in the equation is simply to demonstrate faith.

The Lord desires to confirm his message of grace to all mankind using ordinary Christians to heal and perform miracles as he did with Paul and Barnabas:

Paul and Barnabas spent considerable time there, speaking boldly for the Lord, who confirmed the message of his grace by enabling them to perform signs and wonders.

ACTS 14:3

There are times when some will mistakenly deny him even though he is present, as in the case of the woman with the issue of blood who touched the edge of his cloak:

As Jesus was on his way, the crowds almost crushed him. And a woman was there who had been subject to bleeding for twelve years, but no one could heal her. She came up behind him and touched the edge of his cloak, and immediately her bleeding stopped. "Who touched me?" Jesus asked. **When they all denied it**, *Peter said, "Master, the people are crowding and pressing against you."*

LUKE 8:43-45 *(Author Emphasis)*

The very people who were there to see Jesus, and were pressing in on him, and even crushing him, denied touching him when asked, "Who touched me?"

Why would they deny touching Jesus? They were believers who would touch Jesus as part of the crowd, but deny touching him when it becomes personal. This is what sometimes happens when Christians are asked to step out of their comfort zone and enter into the miraculous or to do something that would stretch their faith.

Two by Two

When Jesus sent out the apostles to the towns and villages, he sent them out two by two, and they *"went from village to village, proclaiming the good news and healing people everywhere"* (Mark 6:7).

Jesus also sent out the second group (the seventy-two), two by two, who returned with joy and said, *"Lord, even the demons submit to us in your name"* (Luke 10:17).

Two is the basic unit for healing (two by two) because it is the number of agreement, and Jesus joins with them to make up the third part of a three-fold cord:

> *Again, truly I tell you that if two of you on earth agree about anything they ask for, it will be done for them by my Father in heaven. For where two or three gather in my name, there am I with them.*
>
> Matthew 18:19-20

> *Though one may be overpowered, two can defend themselves. A cord of three strands is not quickly broken.*
>
> Ecclesiastes 4:12

> TWO IS THE BASIC UNIT FOR HEALING BECAUSE IT IS THE NUMBER OF AGREEMENT

When two are in agreement in praying for the sick, Jesus is with us forming the third person of the three-fold cord; it is *"Christ in us the hope of glory"* (Colossians 1:27).

It would be a good strategy for the church to send out their people two by two to proclaim the Gospel and heal the sick. This is a basic strategy that Jesus did when he sent out the first disciples into the towns and villages. Jehovah Witnesses go door to door with empty words. Why shouldn't Christians go door to door with the truth and a demonstration of the Holy Spirit's power?

This is an evangelistic strategy for a team of two, so it doesn't take many, but a church could have many teams of two. However the team of two concept is important, because Jesus did it when he sent out the first groups into the ministry; besides he will work with us to form a three-fold cord.

HIS TEAM

When Jesus started his ministry after being baptized, he preached about the Kingdom, but he didn't do any miracles (Matthew 4:17-19) until he called his first disciples. It was when he had a team that he began to do miracles. We are included in that team, a team that keeps expanding.

When we follow the model and strategies of Scripture we will have success. In John 21:3-6, Peter and some of the others went fishing; they got into the boat, but that night they caught nothing. Jesus called from the shore and asked if they caught any fish, but they had not. He told them to throw their net on the right side of the boat, and when they did, they were unable to haul the net in because of the large number of fish.

The same is true today. When we use the strategy he has given us, we will discover that it is the most effective strategy imaginable.

In the heavenly connection, Jesus does what he sees the Father doing; he then tells us to do the same, and fills us with power and authority, so we are equipped to do it. He then says that he will work with us from heaven, so the will of the Father would be carried out.

THE FATHER STARTED IT

Jesus only did what he saw the Father doing, so the Father modeled healing for Jesus; then Jesus modeled it for us:

> *The Son can do nothing by himself; he can do only what he sees his Father doing, because whatever the Father does the Son also does. For the Father loves the Son and shows him all he does.*
>
> JOHN 5:19-20

Miracles point upward to the one sitting on the throne, the Father to whom we give all the glory.

The miracles done by Jesus were also what convinced a member of the Jewish ruling council that Jesus was the Son of God:

> *Now there was a Pharisee, a man named Nicodemus who was a member of the Jewish ruling council. He came to Jesus at night and said, "Rabbi, we know that you are a teacher who has come from God. For no one could perform the signs you are doing if God were not with Him."*
>
> JOHN 3:1-2

Nicodemus was among the religious elite of the day, and yet through the miracles he witnessed, he was convinced that the man from Galilee was from the Father.

Some Pharisees and teachers of the law were thinking to themselves that Jesus had no authority to forgive sin, but Jesus knowing their thoughts said:

> *Why are you thinking these things in your hearts? Which is easier: to say, "Your sins are forgiven," or to say, "Get up and walk?" But I want you to know that the Son of Man has authority on earth to forgive sins. So he said to the paralyzed man, "I tell you, get up, take your mat and go home." Immediately he stood up in front of them, took what he had been lying on and went home praising God.*
>
> LUKE 5:22-25

To paraphrase what Jesus said, if he could heal the paralytic, it was proof that he could also forgive sin because he had authority from the Father.

It is through signs, wonders, and miracles that the Father confirms his Word to an unbelieving world, and it is the most powerful strategy the church can have in carrying out the Great Commission:

> *For if the word spoken through angels proved unalterable, and every transgression and disobedience received a just penalty, how will we escape if we neglect so great a salvation? After it was first spoken through the Lord, it was confirmed to us by those who heard, God also testifying with them, both by signs and wonders and by various miracles and by gifts of the Holy Spirit according to his own will.*
>
> HEBREWS 2:2-4

Also, Peter got up on the day of Pentecost after being baptized in the Holy Spirit and declared:

> *Fellow Israelites, listen to this: Jesus of Nazareth was a man accredited by God to you by miracles, wonders, and signs, which God did among you through him, as you yourselves know.*
>
> ACTS 2:22

Again we see that miracles, signs, and wonders are used in authenticating the Gospel message of Jesus Christ.

To settle a theological dispute as to whether the Gentiles could be saved, Paul and Barnabas told the apostles and elders from the Jerusalem church about the miracles that were done among the Gentiles:

> *The whole assembly became silent as they listened to Barnabas and Paul telling about the signs and wonders God had done among the Gentiles through them.*
>
> ACTS 15:12

Paul and Barnabas offered the miracles done among the Gentiles as proof that God had called the Gentiles to salvation. The apostles, knowing that only God could do miracles, accepted that as proof that salvation had come to the Gentiles.

Because Jesus healed the sick, a large number of people believed; this is what consistently happened:

> *Jesus did many other miraculous signs in the presence of his disciples, which are not recorded in this book. But these are written that you may believe that Jesus is the Christ, the Son of God, and that by believing you may have life in his name.*
>
> JOHN 20:30-31

Miracles from the Father helped the early church to become established; I can't imagine the church having the success it did without signs, wonders, and miracles.

ANOINT WITH OIL

Scripture says that when we pray for the sick, we should anoint with oil:

> *Call the elders of the church to pray over him and anoint him with oil in the name of the Lord.*
>
> JAMES 5:14

I had difficulty understanding this Scripture because Jesus never anointed with oil when he prayed for the sick, and it is only mentioned a few times being used by the disciples. There are a few occasions where Jesus spit on someone, anointing them with his own spit. I would have to say that when Jesus used his spit in place of oil, it represented a type of anointing oil, or a type of Holy Spirit. My understanding of this is that oil is optional. From experience, I have not found any difference in using oil or not using it. But the Bible does say to call the elders and anoint with oil, so you can draw your own conclusions about using oil. I would say that it is more about anointing with the Holy Spirit.

> *After he took him aside, away from the crowd, Jesus put his fingers into the man's ears. Then he spit and touched the man's tongue.*
>
> MARK 7:33

> *He took the blind man by the hand and led him outside the village. When he had spit on the man's eyes and put his hands on him, Jesus asked, "Do you see anything?"*
>
> MARK 8:23

> *Having said this, he spit on the ground, made some mud with the saliva, and put it on the man's eyes.*
>
> JOHN 9:6

Jesus' spit is a type of anointing oil, and I would conclude that both Jesus' spit, and anointing oil are a type and shadow of the Holy Spirit. It is the Holy Spirit who heals, and he is always present when there is healing.

The disciples used oil occasionally as mentioned in Mark 6:7-13:

Calling the twelve to him, he sent them out two by two and gave them authority over evil spirits ... They went out and preached that people should repent. They drove out many demons and anointed many sick people with oil and healed them.

But the disciples' most prominent healings were done without oil, and in a few instances, in the most outrageous ways:

- In Acts 5:15 Peter's shadow healed people in the streets;
- In Acts 19:11-12, Paul used handkerchiefs and aprons to heal people;
- In Acts 3, Peter and John healed a crippled beggar at the gate called Beautiful without the use of oil.

In the majority of healing cases there is no mention of oil being used. I would conclude that the use of oil is optional, and not something to be done as a ritual.

Keep Your Healing

One of the great disappointments in the healing ministry is when someone, after being healed, loses their healing. To get a healing or to keep a healing is a responsibility to take seriously and aggressively. We are to resist ailments, diseases, wounds, and accidents, in the same way that we resist the devil, as it says in Revelation 3:11:

Hold on to what you have.

The devil will try to rob you of your blessing.

Some people are like seed along the path, where the word is sown. As soon as they hear it, Satan comes and takes away the word that was sown in them.

Our testimony is a major factor in keeping our healing, and Revelation 12:11 gives us a clear understanding of this. It says:

They triumphed over him by the blood of the Lamb and by the word of their testimony.

We have victory over the devil by the blood of the Lamb, Jesus Christ, the Lamb of God. In conjunction with the blood of the Lamb, we must use our testimony. Our testimony is that Jesus has healed us—it has already happened. It is in the past tense. Notice, "by his wounds you **have been** healed" (1 Peter 2:24). So, our testimony would sound something like this: "In Jesus' name I **have been** healed," or "In Jesus' name **I am** healed."

> WE HAVE VICTORY OVER THE DEVIL BY THE BLOOD OF THE LAMB AND THE WORD OF OUR TESTIMONY

When Jesus healed the Gadarene demoniac, he wanted to travel with Jesus, but Jesus told him, "Go home to your own people and tell them how much the Lord has done for you, and how he has had mercy on you" (Mark 5:19). This is basically the man giving a testimony, which was a great benefit to him, as well as a benefit to the people who heard it. As the man went throughout the region, he proclaimed the Gospel, and received the blessing of giving his testimony.

When we testify to what God has done, it builds us up as well as those who hear it, and through it, we keep what God has given us.

I had some terrific meetings in a church where I imparted the gift of healing to a team of leaders, and many people were healed through them including people coming out of wheelchairs, walkers, and discarding their canes. After a couple weeks had passed, I spoke to the pastor and he told me that many people had lost their healing. The first thing that I wanted to know was about their testimony: Were they allowed to give testimony in church, and were they repeating their testimony when they felt any inkling of their sickness coming back? The answer was no, so I felt very disappointed for the people, who could have easily kept their healing with a thing as simple as giving their testimony publicly and telling it to the devil when he came to put the sickness back on them.

When someone is healed, they are like Peter when he was walking on water. He was okay *as long as he was looking at Jesus,* but when he started looking at the wind and waves he began to sink. Wind and waves are elements of the world and if we look at them, we will sink, but if we keep our eyes on Jesus we will be victorious. The world and its elements are the enemy of faith. If we believe what the world has to say about healing or signs, wonders, and miracles, we then will have no faith for healing.

This is why we are tested in the same way that Jesus was tested (Matthew 4:1-11):

- the desires of the flesh test,
- the desires of the eyes test,
- and pride in possessions test (1 John 2:16).

These are faith destroyers and could keep you from being healed or cause you to lose your healing.

If you start getting symptoms of your illness coming back, the thing to do is aggressively come against it. Remember with just a little faith we can speak to a mountain and it will move (Matthew 17:20-21). Speak to those symptoms and they will move, but be aggressive! If you received your healing at church or home group, the minute you walk out the door, the world is going to start speaking to you with its negatives.

The message from the world comes from the father of lies, but listen how Jesus describes him:

> *He was a murderer from the beginning, and has nothing to do with the truth, because there is no truth in him. When he lies, he speaks out of his own character, for he is a liar and the father of lies.*
>
> JOHN 8:44

This is a spiritual struggle that we are in, but the truth is that you will easily win this battle because of the weapons that God has given you.

I live in Texas, which is very hot in the summer. If I have the time, I'll go play a round of golf. I don't care how hot it is, I love to walk the golf course. It could be over 100 degrees and I will still walk. I was walking the course one time and all of a sudden I felt like I was going to pass out from heat stroke. It was mid-day, and I was playing alone. What did I do? I began taking authority over the heat (the mountain), and just kept walking. I felt woozy, but I kept taking authority. I took about ten steps and I started to feel better and within ten more steps I felt fine. This has happened to me about a dozen different times, where I felt this nauseating feeling from the Texas sun beating down on me. As I took authority in the name of Jesus, I completely recovered and finished the round of golf without difficulty. I became very confident in what would happen; it was almost like a game that the enemy would attack me with the heat and I would take authority over it in Jesus' name.

This is something that we all can do. Don't let the devil put junk on you—don't take it. You can overcome him by resisting him.

Resist the devil, and he will flee from you.

JAMES 4:7

This means that whenever you resist anything the devil is trying to put on you, you are resisting him. So if you experience any sudden attack on your physical body such as flu-like symptoms, heat stroke, heart problems, etc., just take authority, and attack back. Don't take it. Be persistent. Don't quit until you have victory.

I recall reading an article in a magazine some years ago about injuries in pro football. It said something to the effect that the average play in the NFL is like being in a car accident. You don't realize it at the time, but it can have long-term effects on the body and brain. Even after playing ten years of pro football, I don't have any health problems. However, every once in a while when I feel a twinge of something in my shoulder, back, knee, or ankle, I immediately begin taking authority to make sure no arthritis sets in and nothing goes wrong. I want to resist those things from causing problems.

Today in the NFL if you have a concussion, they will take you out of the game—even if it doesn't appear to be severe. They thoroughly examine the player in any situation of injury. Early in my career while playing tight end, I jumped for a pass over the middle; I caught it and came down on my head. When I went back to the huddle, our quarterback, Jack Kemp (later known as Congressman Kemp) called the next play. As we broke the huddle, I had to ask Jack "What do I do?" He knew that

I was dingy (that is what we called being concussed back then), and he told me what to do. Coming off the field, I heard him say to the coach, "Paul's dingy." The trainer and doctor brought me to the bench and asked me the defining questions that would determine if I could go back in the game or not: (1) How many fingers do I have up? (2) What day is it? They gave me the okay to go back in the game, and as I was on the sideline waiting for the offense to go back on the field, I heard Jack say to the coach, "What do I do about Paul, he doesn't know the plays?" The coach responded, "So, tell him." And I played the rest of the game with a concussion; I had to be told my assignment on every play as we broke the huddle on the way to the line of scrimmage. I will continue to trust God that there are no ill effects from football.

James warns us about being double minded, which is listening to what the Scriptures say, then listening to the message of the world.

> *Let him ask in faith, with no doubting, for the one who doubts is like a wave of the sea that is driven and tossed by the wind. For that person must not suppose that he will receive anything from the Lord; he is a double-minded man, unstable in all his ways.*
>
> JAMES 1:6-8

Hezekiah prayed for himself. God healed him, added fifteen years to his life, and delivered him from the Assyrian King (2 Kings 20:1-7). Praying for oneself for healing can be done effectively, but praying for a family member or someone close to you, usually takes persistence. Do you trust God with your soul? If so, then you can also trust him with your body. If he will heal your soul, he will also heal your body. You can appropriate healing for yourself and for others. Any Christian can do it! The average Christian is more than capable of healing the sick, being healed, and keeping their healing.

The Bible is clear that we can pray for the sick. When we are the sick person, we can pray and expect to be healed. Scripture says to lay hands on the sick and they will get well (Mark 16:18). This includes praying for yourself.

> Lay hands on the sick and they will get well— this includes praying for yourself

Chapter Four

Commissioned, Commanded, Empowered

Jesus knew that at some point he would leave this earth, and his work on earth, as a man, would be done. But how could his work on earth continue if he were leaving? The apostles and disciples who were chosen were ordinary men and women, mostly uneducated, simple folks. However, Jesus commissioned (commanded), and empowered these ordinary men and women, his disciples, to do the very same things that he had been doing.

The definition of a ***commission*** is a formal warrant granting the power to perform various acts or duties.[1]

This is a fairly accurate definition of the commissioning Jesus gave us, which is the granting of power to perform various acts or duties.

Jesus made it clear that when he chose his followers, he did not necessarily choose the wise, the scholar, or the philosopher. Instead he chose the foolish things, the lowly things, the despised things—and the things that are not—to nullify the things that are, so that no one may boast before Him (1 Corinthians 1:20-26).

Even though he specifically chose foolish things, that doesn't mean that we remain foolish things, because the Holy Spirit in us, will work with us to make dramatic improvements.

It's interesting that there are many Scriptures about healing, and none of them exclude any Christian from healing the sick, young, old, male, or female, foolish thing, lowly thing, despised thing, etc., nor do they limit the extent of power that each Christian can have. We all have the same amount of power from the same power source.

Jesus commissioned his disciples:

Go into all the world and preach the good news to all creation. Whoever believes and is baptized will be saved, but whoever does not believe will be condemned. And these signs will accompany those who believe: In my name they will drive out demons; they will speak in new tongues; they will pick up snakes with their hands; and when they drink deadly poison, it will not hurt them at all; they will place their hands on sick people, and **they will get well.**

MARK 16:15-18 *(Author emphasis)*

Notice it says, "they will place their hands on sick people, and they will get well." Jesus says that **they will … they will**. "They will place their hands on sick people, and they will get well."

Jesus gives a matter of fact commission to go and heal the sick. This is a commissioning for all believers, and it doesn't sound like it is optional.

Do you have a faith that will allow you to heal the sick? If you're a Christian, you do. Healing is cut and dry—it is supposed to happen. God wants it to happen, and he wants it to happen through you. "Those who believe" includes anyone with faith: young or old, male or female, etc.

If we were to join the verses in Mark 16 (17 and 18b), it would read like this:

These signs will accompany those who believe ... they will place their hands on sick people, and they will get well.

It doesn't say these signs **might** accompany those who believe, or they **might** get well. It essentially says that believers **will** heal the sick:

They **will** place their hands on sick people, and they **will** get well.

The ministry of the miraculous is for "those who believe," and it is not based on one's gifting, but primarily on one's faith.

Preaching, teaching, and healing the sick are unquestionable principles of Scripture. They are principles of Jesus' ministry, and in the commissioning of his disciples. Jesus commissioned his disciples to participate in the same ministry that he did, and gave them specific instructions:

As you go, preach this message: "The Kingdom of heaven is near. Heal the sick, raise the dead, cleanse those who have leprosy, drive out demons. Freely you have received, freely give."

MATTHEW 10:7-8

In Luke 9:1, Jesus gathered his apostles and gave them power and authority to drive out all demons and heal diseases.

Then in Luke 10:1, he did the same thing with the seventy-two. Jesus sent them out ahead of him; they went and ministered, and they all came back with this same testimony:

Lord, even the demons submit to us in your name.

LUKE 10:17

Jesus sent the whole group to minister in his name, and they all returned from ministering, having total victory. There were no stragglers who said, "Well, I tried, but it didn't work for me." They were all sent and they all came back declaring victory over demons, which brings healing.

When the seventy-two returned from ministering, Jesus reassured them saying:

> *I saw Satan fall like lightning from heaven. I have given you authority to trample on snakes and scorpions and to overcome all the power of the enemy; nothing will harm you.*
>
> LUKE 10:18-19

Jesus, speaking to the group of seventy-two, gave them authority over all the power of the enemy. Jesus gave them unlimited authority against Satan and his demons, and also in the same verse he gives unlimited protection by saying "Nothing will harm you."

The requirement to do the work of God is simply to believe in the One that he sent—Jesus Christ! Simple child-like faith is the first and foremost requirement. It is not by our own power of godliness, but by belief in the Son of God.

The latter rain is a time of signs and wonders for old and young alike. It will be a time like no other in terms of harvesting. It will be a greater time of healing and miracles than in the early church because the latter will be greater than the former. And that latter time is now; every Christian is part of it.

The examples of Jesus preaching the Kingdom, healing the sick, and commissioning his disciples, are unquestionably a principle for the church. Jesus clearly commissions believers to heal the sick, and it isn't a select few, but all his disciples.

In 2 Corinthians 12:12 Paul says, "I persevered in demonstrating among you the marks of a true apostle, including signs, wonders, and miracles." I want to clear up this point.

Paul is saying a true apostle will have signs, wonders, and miracles in their ministry; however, this does not mean that every person who does signs, wonders, and miracles is an apostle. According to the Scriptures, signs, wonders, and miracles are for all who believe (Acts 6:8, Mark 16:17). What Paul is saying would eliminate the claims of a false apostle because of a lack of signs, wonders, and miracles.

> SIGNS, WONDERS, AND MIRACLES ARE FOR ALL WHO BELIEVE

It is clear that when Jesus called and commissioned his disciples and apostles to preach, he also called and commissioned them to drive out demons and heal the sick.

They went out and preached that people should repent. They drove out many demons and anointed many sick people with oil and healed them.

Stephen had recently been chosen as a deacon whose duty, as a deacon, was to wait on tables. The Bible records:

> *Stephen, a man full of God's grace and power, did great wonders and miraculous signs among the people.*
>
> ACTS 6:8

He was a deacon who did great wonders and miraculous signs, but he was not an apostle; he was a deacon who waited on tables. If signs, wonders, and miracles are missing in the ministry of an apostle, it would do more to disqualify them as a true apostle.

In Isaiah 53, the Father commissioned Jesus to preach the Word and heal the sick. So when Jesus began his ministry, one of the first things he did was to go into the synagogue and tell the people about his commission from the Father:

> *He went to Nazareth, where he had been brought up, and on the Sabbath day he went into the synagogue, as was his custom. And he stood up to read. The scroll of the prophet Isaiah was handed to him. Unrolling it, he found the place where it is written:*
>
> *"The Spirit of the Lord is on me, because he has anointed me to preach good news to the poor. He has sent me to proclaim freedom for the prisoners and recovery of sight for the blind, to release the oppressed, to proclaim the year of the Lord's favor."*
>
> LUKE 4:16-19

Just as Jesus was commissioned by the Father to preach the Good News and heal the sick, he likewise commissioned his disciples. The result of that commission was that they "went from village to village, preaching the Gospel and healing people everywhere" (Luke 9:6).

WE ARE COMMANDED

When Jesus commissioned believers to heal the sick, it should also be taken as a command to heal the sick.

Jesus sent out his disciples with the following instructions (Matthew 10:7-8):

- As you go, preach this message: "The Kingdom of heaven is near."

- Heal the sick.

- Raise the dead.

- Cleanse those who have leprosy.

- Drive out demons.

- Freely you have received, freely give.

Jesus' instructions were, "As you go," not if you go, or when you go. He gave the command, "as you go," do the following things: "Heal the sick, raise the dead, cleanse those who have leprosy, drive out demons." This is not only a commissioning, but also a clear command.

When Jesus sent out the seventy-two (Luke 10:8), his instructions were:

- When you enter a town and are welcomed, eat what is offered to you.

- Heal the sick who are there.

- Tell them, "The Kingdom of God has come near to you."

So when he said that we would do these things, he is certainly speaking about the two primary things he did everywhere he went. This is the model he left with us—commissioned and commanded us to follow. Jesus said:

I tell you the truth, anyone who has faith in me will do what I have been doing. He will do even greater things than these, because I am going to the Father.

JOHN 14:12

Was Jesus mistaken when he said this? Of course not. Jesus was not mistaken, but the church has not yet fully entered into the greater things ministry, because "greater things" will require that there be healing and miracles to accompany the preaching and teaching of the Word. The statement by Jesus, "they will do even greater things than these," is the prophetic destiny of the church. The whole church!

Jesus said that these signs will accompany those who believe. He didn't say, "these signs **might** accompany those who believe." He said, "They **will** place their hands on sick people, and they **will** get well."

We have to look at healing differently. It is a non-optional command for the body of Christ—not for the few, but for every believer in every church. It is a command; it is not optional. It is the strategy that Jesus gave for an incredible harvest of souls, and to crush Satan.

When God gives us a command in his Word, it is pretty direct. For this reason, we have no trouble understanding that the Ten Commandments are really commandments: You shall not murder, you shall not commit adultery, you shall not steal, you shall not give false testimony, etc. In the same way, healing is a command, we should have no trouble understanding this.

The Ten Commandments were inscribed on tablets of stone on the mountain by the finger of God (Deuteronomy 9:10), yet there are many more commandments in the Bible. Though given in a less dramatic way than inscription on stone by the finger of God, they are still commandments and carry as much weight as the Ten Commandments.

It doesn't sound like Jesus is only giving a suggestion when he says, "as you go" in Matthew 10:7. It is said in such a matter-of-fact way, it's like he was saying, "Go brush your teeth, wash your face, and change your underwear." He doesn't qualify it by saying, "Those of you who have the appropriate healing gift, might want to heal the sick and raise the dead." But he gives the command for all believers to "go, preach this message: The Kingdom of Heaven is near. Heal the sick, raise the dead, cleanse those who have leprosy, drive out demons. Freely you have received, freely give."

He called and sent those he designated as apostles (Mark 3:13-15):

Jesus went up on a mountainside and called to him those he wanted, and they came to him. He appointed twelve—designating them apostles that they might be with him and that he might send them out to preach and to have authority to drive out demons.

Some things to take note of from this passage:

- They were the first apostles.

- Jesus sent them out for the first time.

- Jesus gave the apostles the first specific instructions about their ministry, which was to preach and drive out demons.

- This is the first time that anyone was given authority. This was so that they would be equipped to carry the battle plan.

To "Heal the sick, raise the dead, cleanse those who have leprosy, drive out demons," is part of message that Jesus sent them with.

Empowered to Heal

We are commissioned to heal the sick; we are commanded to heal the sick; and we are also empowered to heal the sick. I think that some might take the availability of God's healing power too lightly, even with skepticism. We read the Scriptures of what is available to us, but then think it's for somebody else, or it's for the super spiritual. The average Christian has more than enough Holy Ghost power to heal the sick.

It is difficult to understand why we don't see more miracles in our churches. the Bible is emphatic in saying that we will receive power:

> *You will receive power when the Holy Spirit comes on you; and you will be my witnesses in Jerusalem, and in all Judea and Samaria, and to the ends of the earth.*
>
> ACTS 1:8

When we receive power, we will then be equipped to be "witnesses in Jerusalem, and in all Judea and Samaria, and to the ends of the earth." But what is this power for? Is it only to preach? Is it only to give a testimony? No! It is to carry out the "greater things" ministry as an extension of the ministry of Jesus. It is to demonstrate the reality of the Gospel of power.

> *I came to you in weakness with great fear and trembling. My message and my preaching were not with wise and persuasive words, but with a demonstration of the Spirit's power, so that your faith might not rest on human wisdom, but on God's power.*
>
> 1 CORINTHIANS 2:3-5

> *Some of you have become arrogant, as if I were not coming to you. But I will come to you very soon, if the Lord is willing, and then I will find out not only how these arrogant people are talking, but what power they have. For the Kingdom of God is not a matter of talk but of power.*
>
> 1 CORINTHIANS 4:18-20

What does it mean to be a witness? Jesus commissioned us to preach and teach the Kingdom and to heal the sick. So to be a witness is to preach and heal, which is the model of Jesus' ministry, and the primary strategy for the church.

The amount of grace the ordinary Christian has is sufficient to serve God in signs, wonders, and miracles.

> *My grace is sufficient for you, for my power is made perfect in weakness.*
>
> 2 Corinthians 12:9

God's grace is sufficient in our weakness, because when we are weak, then God's power is able to take over. God is sufficient; that is what God told Moses in Exodus 3:14. He said, "I am who I am," which means, God is what we need him to be.

Greater Things

Jesus guaranteed his ministry would continue after he left the earth by making this promise:

> *Believe me when I say that I am in the Father and the Father is in me; or at least believe on the evidence of the works themselves. Very truly I tell you, whoever believes in me will do the works I have been doing, and they will do even greater things than these, because I am going to the Father.*
>
> John 14:11-12

A greater things ministry is not something which only the select few super-spiritual can enter into; it is for all Christians. It will happen because Jesus is going to the Father and when Jesus goes to the Father, he is going to send the Holy Spirit (John 15:26). We will receive the Holy Spirit, the spirit of power, to carry out a "greater things" ministry which began on the Day of Pentecost. He promised that after he ascended into Heaven, he would work with us to continue signs, wonders, and miracles (Mark 16:20):

> *Then the disciples went out and preached everywhere, and the Lord worked with them and confirmed his Word by the signs that accompanied it.*

The believer can be confident in coming into a "greater things" ministry because 1) Jesus sent the Holy Spirit, and 2) he works with believers as he sits on his throne in Heaven.

After the baptism in the Holy Spirit, we see a transformation as he enters a "greater things" ministry (Acts 5:12-16):

> *The apostles performed many signs and wonders among the people. And all the believers used to meet together in Solomon's Colonnade. No one else dared join them, even though they were highly regarded by the people. Nevertheless, more and more men and women believed in the Lord and were added to their number. As a result, people brought the sick into the streets and laid them on beds and mats so that at least Peter's shadow might fall on some of them as he passed by. Crowds gathered also from the towns around Jerusalem, bringing their sick and those tormented by impure spirits, and all of them were healed.*

Although Peter's shadow healed people and raised the dead as he walked by, (Acts 9:41-42), he still had issues in his life; he was accused of being a hypocrite and fearful:

> *Before certain men came from James, he used to eat with the Gentiles. But when they arrived, he began to draw back and separate himself*

from the Gentiles because he was afraid of those who belonged to the circumcision group. The other Jews joined him in his hypocrisy, so that by their hypocrisy even Barnabas was led astray.

GALATIANS 2:12-13

Peter, even with having issues of fear and hypocrisy, was still able to enter into a "greater things" ministry.

Peter's development into a "greater things" ministry didn't happen overnight. He progressed because he spent time with Jesus, watched what Jesus did, followed his teaching, saw how he died, saw him after the resurrection, and was there when the tongues of fire fell upon the disciples. Peter matured over time, and came into the healing anointing of "greater things" through a process of faith building.

> DEVELOPMENT INTO A "GREATER THINGS" MINISTRY REQUIRES A PROGRESSION OF RELATIONSHIP WITH JESUS

The "greater things" ministry doesn't mean that we will each have a greater healing ministry than Jesus, but it does mean that collectively, as his Body, and as he works with us from Heaven, we can enter a "greater things" ministry collectively.

Philip the evangelist entered the "greater things" ministry:

When the crowds heard Philip and saw the signs he performed, they all paid close attention to what he said. For with shrieks, impure spirits came out of many, and many who were paralyzed or lame were healed. So there was great joy in that city.

ACTS 8:6-8

There are numerous examples of the signs, wonders, and miracles after the day of Pentecost. In fact, the New Testament says that they reached the entire world using Jesus' model of ministry. The disciples were commissioned, commanded, and empowered to carry out this model of ministry—the greater things' ministry—and Jesus worked with them as the Holy Spirit worked through them and they reached the entire world.

> *I thank my God through Jesus Christ for all of you, because your faith is being reported* **all over the world.**
>
> ROMANS 1:8 *(Author Emphasis)*

> *Faith comes from hearing the message, and the message is heard through the Word about Christ. But I ask: "Did they not hear?" Of course they did: Their voice has* **gone out into all the earth,** *their words to the ends of the world*
>
> ROMANS 10:18-19 10 *(Author Emphasis)*

> *You have already heard in the true message of the Gospel that has come to you. In the same way, the Gospel is bearing fruit and growing* **throughout the whole world**
>
> COLOSSIANS 1:5-6 *(Author Emphasis)*

> *Do not move from the hope held out in the Gospel. This is the Gospel that you heard and that has been* **proclaimed to every creature under Heaven,** *and of which I, Paul, have become a servant*
>
> COLOSSIANS 1:23 *(Author Emphasis)*

The "greater things'" ministry was in full effect and spreading all over the world "by the power of signs and wonders, through the power of the Spirit of God" (Romans 15:19).

The church is progressing to become the church without spot or wrinkle. From the time of Martin Luther (1511 A.D., when he had a revelation of salvation), and especially in the last century (the 1900s), the five-fold ministry (apostles, prophets, evangelists, pastors, and teachers) went through the beginning of a restoration, and now as those ministries mature, what must also mature is the ministry model that Jesus used.

When Does "All" Happen?

The "greater things" ministry could eventually evolve into the healing of "all." The "greater things" ministry begins for believers when Jesus goes to the Father:

Whoever believes in me will do the works I have been doing, and they will do even greater things than these, because I am going to the Father.

JOHN 14:12

Because Jesus has gone to the Father, believers have already entered the "greater things" ministry that Jesus mentions.

However, the healing of "all" that we see in the ministry of Jesus, Peter, and Paul, is for a time when we "all reach unity in the faith and in the knowledge of the Son of God and become mature, attaining to the whole measure of the fullness of Christ."

Jesus healed **all** who came to him; some of the disciples also healed all:

*He went about doing good and healing **all** who were oppressed by the devil.*

ACTS 10:38 *(Author Emphasis)*

> *He cast out spirits with a word and healed **all** who were sick.*
>
> MATTHEW 8:16 *(Author Emphasis)*

> *I have given you authority to trample on snakes and scorpions and to overcome **all** the power of the enemy.*
>
> LUKE 10:19 *(Author Emphasis)*

> *Crowds gathered also from the towns around Jerusalem, bringing their sick and those tormented by impure spirits, and **all** of them were healed.*
>
> ACTS 5:16 *(Author Emphasis)*

This will happen, as we mature in faith and knowledge according to Ephesians 4:13:

> *Until we all reach unity in the faith and in the knowledge of the Son of God and become mature, attaining to the **whole measure of the fullness of Christ**.*

As the Body of Christ continues to reach unity in the faith, we will attain to the whole measure of the fullness of Christ. When this happens we will fully come into the "greater things" ministry where "all" will be healed. We will then see that we will overcome "all" the power of the enemy, all the time. At the present time we are seeing an escalation of signs, wonders, and miracles through the Body of Christ that will continue to grow, and it will be even greater that what we see in the book of Acts because the latter will be greater than the former.

Many have been part of great meetings when all were healed, but we have not yet seen it where all were healed all the time. Until then, we will still see a vast number of the sick being healed.

It's Better that I Go

It is for your good that I am going away.

John 16:7

Jesus knew that he was going to the cross, and then going back to the Father. However, the disciples probably could not imagine what could be better than to have Jesus remain with them.

If Jesus were still on earth, it wouldn't take faith for us to believe in him. Everyone on the earth would have acknowledged who he is. He would be the leader of leaders. Few would doubt His supremacy in all things. He would have been alive for two thousand years now, and that alone would convince people of who he is. He would still be healing all who needed it, he would be settling disputes between nations, he would automatically be drafted as the president of the governing body of the world. He would have 24-hour full media coverage with every move he made, as he went about teaching and healing. His truth could not be questioned, and he would have control of the world's wealth, politics, etc.

However, when Satan (Lucifer) was thrown out of Heaven, one-third of the angels fell with him. Satan must have had a lot of influence over those angels since one-third of them fell with him. The angels thrown out of Heaven must have believed Satan rather than God. If Satan had that much influence in Heaven, he probably would have that much influence here on earth. But the promise of Scripture is that Satan will be defeated in the end:

The God of peace will soon crush Satan under your feet.

Romans 16:20

God sent the Holy Spirit, and through the Holy Spirit we will reign supreme because of "greater works," which is certainly enough to crush Satan.

Greater things, means that we are included today in all that Jesus did. We can do what he did in his ministry of signs, wonders, and miracles.

The Body of Christ has waited for the harvest to come in, and it seems that we are getting close. The harvesting has begun in unprecedented numbers in some places around the world. However, like the farmer, we must be patient for the harvest to begin working in our country with God working through us:

> *Be patient, then, brothers, until the Lord's coming. See how the farmer waits for the land to yield its valuable crop and how patient he is for the autumn and spring rains.*
>
> JAMES 5:7

We are entering a time of harvest knowing that the church will do greater things, as Jesus said we would do. He is pouring out His Spirit on all flesh—we are commissioned, commanded, and empowered to heal the sick; we will crush the head of Satan. All these promises, and more, are for us, his Body.

ENDNOTE

1. *Merriam-Webster's Deluxe Dictionary: Tenth Collegiate Edition.* 10th ed. New York: Reader's Digest Assn., 1998. Print.

Chapter Five

Just Do It

I ministered at a service for a prison in Texas where many inmates had never been to a church. I think the reason this particular group was in our meeting was that their cells were being searched and the prison staff put them in the sanctuary to get them out of the way. After the message, we called for those who needed to be healed. They were reluctant to come forward, but eventually a few began trickling down. As they were healed, we asked them to tell everyone in the meeting what happened to them. Almost every one of them said, "I don't really believe in this stuff …" but they assured everyone present that they had really been healed of something. Two men stand out in my mind because they had tatoos covering even their faces and heads. They too spoke first of their unbelief, but then gave a testimony about receiving healing—convincing testimony. They did their best to coax their fellow inmates to come forward for healing. Some did, and they were healed as well.

Many went from total unbelief to faith in the living God. Why? These street thugs were touched by a demonstration of the healing power of

God. No persuasion from even the most gifted preacher could ever be as convincing as an undeniable experience with God.

The really exciting thing about the meeting was that it was other prisoners who did the healing. They were novices with no theological background or training. They had the gift of healing imparted to them, and they laid hands on those who came forward and healed them. It was beautiful!

We ended the meeting with a call for salvation and many came forward and found a new hope, and relevance in their existence.

We take for granted that as long as we have enough faith to get to Heaven, everything is okay—this is all that is required of us. But God is looking for a much higher standard of faith than getting saved and waiting around to go to Heaven.

Every Christian church should have a culture of power—signs, wonders, and miracles—but instead we have many Bible clubs. These are fellowships and churches whose level of faith is minimal. God is looking for extraordinary faith that does something: healing, miracles, casting out demons, picketing at abortion clinics, feeding the poor, etc. Faith without works is dead!

In the book of Matthew, a man brought his son to Jesus for healing, and he complained to Jesus, "I brought him to your disciples, but they could not heal him."

This sounds like a complaint we would hear today. With every move of God there is always a segment of the church that will not move forward. Regardless of what God is doing, they will remain in their comfort zone. God is moving today, demonstrating his power in order to authenticate the Gospel.

Paul states it concisely:

My message and my preaching were not with wise and persuasive words, but with a demonstration of the Spirit's power, so that your faith might not rest on human wisdom, but on God's power.

1 Corinthians 2:4-5

The Gospel is not like any other religion; it is full of power for all who believe.

Jesus praised the Father for hiding healing and deliverance from the wise and learned (unbelievers), and even some churches (Bible clubs), but revealing it instead to the children of God:

At that time Jesus, full of joy through the Holy Spirit, said, "I praise you, Father, Lord of Heaven and earth, because **you have hidden these things from the wise and learned,** *and revealed them to little children. Yes, Father, for this is what you were pleased to do."*

Luke 10: 18-21 *(Author Emphasis)*

We are called to demonstrate him, and not just with wise and persuasive words. It will take wise and persuasive words validated by a demonstration of God's power to subdue the earth. Like my buddy, Apostle John Kelly says: "We need to be seeker friendly until the music starts," which means the worship has to be dynamic, the message has to be dynamic, and there has to be a demonstration of God's power. America has the greatest preachers in the world, but we also need signs, wonders, and miracles in order to reach the world.

There are all flavors of churches, and we can choose any flavor we like. You can be any flavor of Christian you like. You can be an irregular attendee, a regular attendee, an inactive member, or an active member. There are even different flavors of deacons and elders. God is looking for attendees, members, deacons and elders who will exercise their faith in building the Kingdom through the gifts and talents that he has given them.

It is no great accomplishment to have faith, because faith without works is dead. Even demons have faith. When the two demon-possessed men saw Jesus on the other side in the region of the Gadarenes, they shouted, "What do you want with us, Son of God?" (Matthew 8:29). That really can't be considered faith because it isn't combined with deeds, but they did at least recognize that Jesus was the Son of God. This is the same level of faith a demon has—a faith that does nothing!

> *You believe that there is one God. Good! Even the demons believe that—and shudder.*
>
> JAMES 2:19

The demons knew more about Jesus than the religious people of the day, more than the Pharisees and Sadducees who refused to believe even when they saw the miracles. This was one group, with a few exceptions, that Jesus' healing and miracles never influenced. It influenced the tax collectors and sinners. It even influenced the demons; at least, the demons pleaded for mercy and acknowledged Jesus as the Son of God.

The Apostle Paul warns about false Christians who are in the ministry for profit or for some other gain that they can get from it:

> *Such people are false apostles, deceitful workers, masquerading as apostles of Christ. And no wonder, for Satan himself masquerades as an angel of light. It is not surprising, then, if his servants also masquerade as servants of righteousness.*
>
> 2 CORINTHIANS 11:13-15

A Pharisee falsely accused Jesus of having a demon in Matthew 12:24:

It is only by Beelzebub, the prince of demons, that this fellow drives out demons.

The religious leader accused Jesus of having a demon when it was he, the Pharisee, who had the demon. Only someone full of demons could accuse the Creator of the universe of having a demon, like the false religious leaders of today, who give a false appearance of piety.

A slave girl, who had an evil spirit, followed Paul. She kept shouting out who they were:

Once when we were going to the place of prayer, this girl followed Paul and the rest of us, shouting ... "These men are servants of the Most High God, who are telling you the way to be saved."

ACTS 16:16-17

The slave girl had a spirit by which she predicted the future, and she earned a great deal of money for her owners by fortune telling. The evil spirit was shouting through the girl, and declaring that Paul and his company were servants of the Most High. It is remarkable that the evil spirit knew more than most of the spiritual leaders of that day.

I was asked to share at a meeting of pastors about the impartation of spiritual gifts. During the break, a gentleman who had been in the ministry for at least 40 years, approached me and asked if I would impart the gift of healing to him? He said that when he started in ministry, he saw healing and miracles at that time, but he started going to a church that didn't believe in miracles and consequently, he lost his gift for healing. Actually, he didn't lose his gift, what he lost was his faith for healing. Since the church (Bible club) where he joined didn't believe in healing, he no longer attempted to heal the sick. Therefore, he no longer saw the sick healed. He lost his faith because of what he had joined.

The church must get out of the Bible club mentality, and get into the attack mode against the evil in society—evil that is causing mayhem in peoples' lives, yes, even in the lives of Christians. Bible clubs won't go to war because they don't feel like they are well equipped for warfare, or even that warfare is necessary. In the worst cases, they believe there is no such thing as spiritual warfare.

Jesus had real concern when he asked this important question, "When the Son of Man comes, will he find faith on the earth?" (Luke 18:8). If he came back today at the time of this writing, I would say that he would find some faith, but not the kind of faith he is really looking for. His standard of faith is far beyond what is on the earth today. We have a lot of folks who have faith for salvation, but Jesus has a higher standard, going beyond salvation.

An example of this is in Matthew 17:14-17:

When they came to the crowd, a man approached Jesus and knelt before Him. "Lord, have mercy on my son," he said. "He has seizures and is suffering greatly. He often falls into the fire or into the water. I brought him to your disciples, but they could not heal him."

"O unbelieving and perverse generation," Jesus replied, "how long shall I stay with you? How long shall I put up with you?"

The crowd that was following Jesus were His disciples and apostles; they were not the random crowds from the towns and countryside. They were the cream of the crop, and if anyone had faith, it was those in that group. Jesus was critical of their lack of faith when they couldn't heal the boy that was brought to Jesus by his father. Jesus wanted a faith that goes beyond faith for salvation. A faith that does the supernatural things of God.

Some Christians don't have a lot of faith because they never do anything that would challenge their faith. We are supposed to walk in faith, and if we do, we will be challenged. Because it is the testing of our faith that causes us to grow:

> *Consider it pure joy, my brothers and sisters, whenever you face trials of many kinds, because you know that the testing of your faith produces perseverance. Let perseverance finish its work so that you may be mature and complete, not lacking anything.*
>
> JAMES 1:2-4

IT IS THE TESTING OF OUR FAITH THAT CAUSES US TO GROW

Some of the apostles that met Jesus after His resurrection, still doubted:

> *Then the eleven disciples went to Galilee, to the mountain where Jesus had told them to go. When they saw him, they worshiped him; but* **some doubted.**
>
> MATTHEW 28:16-17 *(Author Emphasis)*

It's incredible that although they saw him, and worshipped him, some of them still doubted. That is a remarkable admission. Here are some of the early disciples looking right at Jesus after his resurrection and still having a difficult time believing the reality and gravity of it all. If some of the disciples who were worshipping him had doubt, what should we think of some of the modern day religious folks who have not even had the evidence of seeing Jesus?

We have a lot of religiosity in Christianity, and religiosity is a faith destroyer. Religion believes in the historical Jesus; it claims that if they were there when Jesus was performing those miracles, they would believe in them. In other words, they don't trust the Word, which is clear about miracles for today.

According to the Scriptures, we are mighty warriors (Ephesians 6:10-18), and in faith we need to act like it. The Lord always sees what we will become, and not our present situation. God wants us to demonstrate His power, and sees us as "strong in the Lord and in his mighty power" (Ephesians 6:10). He doesn't see us in our present situation, but in a place of strength where he wants to bring us.

These are troubling times. There is more difficulty in society today than ever before experienced. We have terrorists and terrorism. We have political stagnation (we can't seem to solve any problems in our society because of the political polarization and political corruption). Sin is more rampant than ever before—promiscuity, evil politicians, pornography, homosexuality, abortion, drugs, crime, wars, terrorism, environmental problems ... you name it!

With all the problems we face, there is a Scripture that gives us a great deal of comfort that our victory is certain:

Where sin increased, grace increased all the more.

ROMANS 5:20-21

In other words, no matter how bad it gets, we, the people of God, will have the grace, authority, and power to overcome.

The early church brought fear to the populace through a display of Holy Ghost power operating through the believers. Today, there is a lot of contempt for the church among unbelievers, and consequently there is no fear of God, but when they see miracles many will fear (respect) God and repent, as in the following Scripture:

> *Some Jews who went around driving out evil spirits tried to invoke the Name of the Lord Jesus over those who were demon-possessed. They would say, "In the name of the Jesus whom Paul preaches, I command you to come out."*
>
> *Seven sons of Sceva, a Jewish chief priest, were doing this. One day the evil spirit answered them, "Jesus I know, and Paul I know about, but who are you?"*
>
> *Then the man who had the evil spirit jumped on them and overpowered them all. He gave them such a beating that they ran out of the house naked and bleeding. When this became known to the Jews and Greeks living in Ephesus,* **they were all seized with fear***, and the name of the Lord Jesus was held in high honor.*
>
> *Many of those who believed now came and openly confessed what they had done. A number who had practiced sorcery brought their scrolls together and burned them publicly. When they calculated the value of the scrolls, the total came to fifty thousand drachmas. In this way the Word of the Lord spread widely and grew in power.*
>
> ACTS 19:13-20 *(Author Emphasis)*

> *Now a man named Ananias, together with his wife Sapphira, also sold a piece of property. With his wife's full knowledge he kept back part of the money for himself, but brought the rest and put it at the apostles' feet.*

Then Peter said, "Ananias, how is it that Satan has so filled your heart that you have lied to the Holy Spirit and have kept for yourself some of the money you received for the land? Didn't it belong to you before it was sold? And after it was sold, wasn't the money at your disposal? What made you think of doing such a thing? You have not lied just to human beings but to God."

When Ananias heard this, he fell down and died. And great fear seized all who heard what had happened. Then some young men came forward, wrapped up his body, and carried him out and buried him.

About three hours later his wife came in, not knowing what had happened. Peter asked her, "Tell me, is this the price you and Ananias got for the land?"

"Yes," she said, "that is the price."

Peter said to her, "How could you conspire to test the Spirit of the Lord? Listen! The feet of the men who buried your husband are at the door, and they will carry you out also."

At that moment she fell down at his feet and died. Then the young men came in and, finding her dead, carried her out and buried her beside her husband. **Great fear seized the whole church** *and all who heard about these events.*

ACTS 5:1-11 *(Author Emphasis)*

A healthy fear of God manifested when God's power was demonstrated. That is what happened in biblical times, and that is what will happen today, as in this story from Mexico City:

I ministered in Mexico City to a church of about one thousand people on a Sunday morning. I asked the pastor to have all the leaders, one hundred of them, seated up front so that I could impart the healing gift to them. I imparted the gift to them and allowed them to minister healing to the people of the church, and as each person was healed they were brought to a microphone to give a testimony. There was a witch in the congregation that morning, and her aim was to disrupt the church service, and/or to curse the minister, the leaders, and the people. However, the witch saw the healing and miracles done by ordinary Christians and feared for her life. So she ran out the door, went home and got all her idols, brought them back to the church and repented. She came back to the church with her large sack of idols while the service was still going on. The following week, the pastor made a display of smashing the idols in front of the whole congregation.

She witnessed the power of God operating through ordinary Christians, and was convinced that she had to repent and turn to Jesus.

Miracles Build Faith

Martha, the sister of Lazarus, declared emphatically that she had faith, but when it came right down to a life and death issue, her faith was only nominal.

> *"Lord," Martha said to Jesus, "if you had been here, my brother would not have died. But I know that even now God will give you whatever you ask."*
>
> *Jesus said to her, "Your brother will rise again."*
>
> *Martha answered, "I know he will rise again in the resurrection at the last day."*
>
> JOHN 11:21-24

In verse 27 she again declared her faith:

"Yes, Lord," she replied, "I believe that you are the Messiah, the Son of God, who is to come into the world."

Martha had a strong faith and openly proclaimed it, but when they were at the tomb where Lazarus was buried her faith faltered. When Jesus asked for the stone blocking the entrance of the cave to be removed, Martha said:

"But, Lord," said Martha, the sister of the dead man, "by this time there is a bad odor, for he has been there four days."

JOHN 11:39

She believed strongly in the resurrection, but when it came to her brother being raised from the dead, her response was locked in the natural reality and she was more concerned about the smell.

Her faith had failed. It is amazing how quickly her faith recovered when Lazarus walked out of the tomb! Many Christians respond the same way to the miraculous. They have no difficulty believing in Jesus, the resurrection, or their own salvation, but have a difficult time with believing for the miraculous.

Jesus told Martha in verse 40:

Did I not tell you that if you believe, you will see the glory of God?"

We witness the glory of God through the miraculous. When we see one, our faith progresses to believe for the next miracle.

Lazarus was dead and rotting when Jesus called him out of the tomb. He walked out under his own power, still in his grave clothes. The crowd outside the tomb had to be totally exhilarated, and filled with joy and faith on seeing Lazarus alive.

The early disciples had their faith strengthened by the miraculous, and so did the irreligious, the religious, and the ignorant. John 2:23 says:

Many believed in his name when they saw the signs he was doing.

With faith the size of a mustard seed, the smallest of garden seeds, we are able to move mountains (Matthew 17:20). Seeds are supposed to grow, that is what seeds do—they are not supposed to stay small forever. The same is true of our faith, it starts small, but is supposed to grow. We go from faith to faith as we fan into flame the gifts within us.

David as a shepherd boy was guarding his flock of sheep. When a lion and then a bear attacked his herd, he killed both of them. So when Israel's army was intimidated by the taunting of the giant Goliath, David drew on his experience of killing the lion and bear and, in faith, he went out and killed the giant. He went from faith to faith, first killing the lion then the bear then killing Goliath.

As we are faithful in times of testing and trials, we go from faith to faith.

His Faith or My Faith?

We never know what obstacles we may run into when praying for the sick. It could be wind and waves, demons, religion, etc.—all of which will try to destroy our faith; however, they can all be overcome.

When Peter tried to walk on water, he didn't sink until he saw the wind and waves (Matthew 14:30). Religion is a faith destroyer because it's only concerned with its tradition and position (Mark 7:13).

It helps if there is an element of faith in the person being prayed for. It doesn't necessarily have to be enormous faith, just a little will do. Yes, it could be a combination of their faith and your faith; it doesn't seem to be one or the other. And in the case where, after prayer, there is not a healing, one cannot play the blame game and decide who didn't exercise faith. Don't put a guilt trip on the person who doesn't get healed. Don't feel like a failure if there isn't a successful healing when you've prayed.

When a detachment of soldiers and some officials from the chief priests and the Pharisees came to arrest Jesus, a person by the name of Malchus, the high priest's servant, was among them. Peter struck Malchus, cutting off his right ear. Jesus healed Malchus. Malchus probably pondered that event for the rest of his life. One moment his ear was on the ground and blood was pouring from the side of his head, and the next moment his ear was re-attached—as if nothing had ever happened.

Malchus wasn't healed because he had faith, he probably didn't have any faith at all, yet he was healed.

JUST DO IT

It's a very simple thing to begin healing the sick. To borrow a slogan that a famous shoe company uses, "Just Do It." That's right, don't wait for the healing evangelist to come to town, or the healing team in your church, or anybody else—just begin doing it in your sphere.

The Good Samaritan (Luke 10:30) probably never encountered someone that needed healing before, and yet he swung into action. Granted this is not healing in a miraculous way, but it is a representative of the healing ministry. When we read the account of the Good Samaritan, it becomes apparent that there is a cost. It requires effort. It requires your time, but if you are willing to pay the price, you will be successful.

I firmly believe that there are Christians who have a gift of healing (authority) or faith for healing and never use it because of fear, insecurity, lack of knowledge, or even just the lack of any encouragement. This is why Paul encouraged Timothy to use to use his gift from God by fanning it into flame (2 Timothy 1:6-7).

Faith overcomes timidity because it releases a spirit of power, love, and of self-discipline. Faith is released by an act of our will.

When we look at the Scriptures where people were used in healing, it seems that no one was excluded, since healing the sick is for all who believe.

> FAITH IS RELEASED BY AN ACT OF OUR WILL

When praying for a sick person, the enemy will originate this thought, "What if nothing happens?" Don't worry if nothing happens—we aren't the ones doing the healing! God will take full responsibility and credit for that. He just wants us to freely give, and in doing so, our faith will grow and our gifts will mature. Healing gifts are given in their embryonic stage; they are not mature yet and won't be mature unless we use them freely. Don't be afraid of making honest mistakes.

Fear will paralyze you and keep you from moving in the miraculous. It's okay for young Christians to take baby steps at first, but it's not okay to take baby steps all our Christian life. Immaturity is never going beyond taking more than baby steps, and that is a hazard in Christianity. Everything in Christianity is meant to grow.

Even Jesus had to mature into the ministry. He had to grow into the Savior who would shed his blood for mankind, it didn't happen overnight.

Jesus grew in wisdom and stature, and in favor with God and men.

LUKE 2:52

If Jesus had to grow in wisdom and stature, how much more do we have to? We grow into our destiny. We grow in the miraculous.

We should be able to identify with everything Jesus did. We are to carry a cross, we will have a resurrection, we will have persecution, we must mature and grow in wisdom, etc.

The path to greater faith and the miraculous is not easy, but it is worth it. Our destiny is determined by our faith. Every hero of the Bible had their faith tested, and they had to pass the tests to go on:

- Joseph was put in jail, but went on;
- Moses faced Pharaoh, but went on;
- David faced Goliath, but went on;
- Peter heard the rooster crow, but went on;
- Jesus faced the cross, but went on.

We won't grow without challenges and failures because it is the testing of our faith that allows us to grow.

AGGRESSIVE FAITH

An aggressive faith will usually pay more dividends than passive faith. A good example of this is the men that tore a roof apart to get their friend in front of Jesus:

Some men came carrying a paralytic on a mat and tried to take him into the house to lay him before Jesus. When they could not find a way to do this because of the crowd, they went up on the roof and lowered him on his mat through the tiles into the middle of the crowd, right in front of Jesus.

When Jesus saw their faith, he said, "Friend, your sins are forgiven."

LUKE 5:18-20

Their friend was on a stretcher. These men could not fight their way through the crowd to get him before Jesus. So they tore the roof apart, removing the tiles so they could lower the stretcher through the roof in front of Jesus. They were not going to be denied, and their aggressive faith got results.

Another example of aggressive faith is the woman who had the bleeding condition (Luke 8:42). Jesus had a crowd pressing in around Him to the point that they were actually almost crushing Him. How could this woman shove, push, and crawl her way to get close enough to touch Jesus? We don't know how she did it, but she did. She displayed an aggressive faith that got her what she wanted—her healing.

We can all have an aggressive faith, and we can all increase the faith that we have. Faith, in one respect, is a lot like forgiveness. We can forgive as an act of our will, and it will eventually become a reality. It is by the sanctifying work of the Holy Spirit that we are able to forgive completely. Faith, like forgiveness, is an act of the will, and the more we can demonstrate faith by works, the more our faith will grow.

Peter had a very powerful healing ministry; even his shadow healed; people (Acts 5:15), but do you think that he had more power than anyone else? No! We all have the same Holy Spirit, and we can all heal the sick, it is a matter of releasing that power and authority through faith. The difference between Peter and some of the others is that he was aggressive. When Peter and John saw the lame beggar at the Gate Beautiful it was Peter who spoke up:

> *Peter looked straight at him, as did John. Then Peter said, "Look at us!"*
>
> *So the man gave them his attention, expecting to get something from them.*
>
> *Then Peter said, "Silver or gold I do not have, but what I do have I give you. In the name of Jesus Christ of Nazareth, walk."*
>
> ACTS 3:4-6

Peter was often the first one to speak, he had an aggressive personality. He was not afraid to step out of the boat, and because he pushed the limit of his faith, he developed an aggressive faith that could heal people.

The Apostle Paul was the same as Peter in terms of having an aggressive faith, although they were quite different in many other ways. In Acts 19:11-12, it says this about Paul:

> *God did extraordinary miracles through Paul, so that even handkerchiefs and aprons that had touched him were taken to the sick, and their illnesses were cured and the evil spirits left them.*

God was able to do extraordinary miracles through Paul because he had the faith to carry God's healing power—even through handkerchiefs and aprons. It's the faith that is the conduit which God uses to do miracles.

Paul, in comparing himself to false apostles, reveals his aggressive faith demonstrated through his works:

> *Are they servants of Christ? (I am out of my mind to talk like this.) I am more. I have worked much harder, been in prison more frequently,*

been flogged more severely, and been exposed to death again and again. Five times I received from the Jews the forty lashes minus one. Three times I was beaten with rods, once I was pelted with stones, three times I was shipwrecked, I spent a night and a day in the open sea, I have been constantly on the move. I have been in danger from rivers, in danger from bandits, in danger from my fellow Jews, in danger from Gentiles; in danger in the city, in danger in the country, in danger at sea; and in danger from false believers.

I have labored and toiled and have often gone without sleep; I have known hunger and thirst and have often gone without food; I have been cold and naked. Besides everything else, I face daily the pressure of my concern for all the churches. Who is weak, and I do not feel weak? Who is led into sin, and I do not inwardly burn?

2 Corinthians 11:23-29

The aggression of Paul is evident in what he lays out about his journey in serving Christ, and he does it with boldness and without reservation.

When someone is praying for the sick, fear, in the many ways it manifests, will try to defeat the gift that is within you, as in the following examples:

- I'll look like an idiot (Yes, you might!)
- Suppose it doesn't work (Don't think about it not working.)
- Only "they" can do it (No, you can!)
- It's not my place (Yes, it is!)
- Too many people are looking (So what?)
- I don't feel anointed (Don't go by how you feel.)

- Maybe I can pray quietly from a distance (No!)
- What will I say? (Keep it simple.)
- I need more practice (This is an opportunity.)

Elijah experienced fear after he challenged and defeated all the prophets of Baal that assembled on Mount Carmel. Jezebel then sent him a message that read:

May the gods deal with me, be it ever so severely, if by this time tomorrow I do not make your life like that of one of them.

1 KINGS 19:2

One would think that Elijah, after the great victory on Mount Carmel would shrug off Jezebel's threatening message, but instead he became fearful and prayed to die:

"I have had enough, Lord," he said. "Take my life; I am no better than my ancestors."

1 KINGS 19:5

This sometimes happens even when you have a particularly anointed time of ministry—the anointing comes off, and we get the blahs. This is what Elijah encountered when the anointing came off him. Instead of that elevated time where the presence of God is strong, we can feel the way Elijah did. It manifested in Elijah as fear, but it effects people differently, sometimes not at all.

The enemy knows we are vulnerable when the anointing comes off after a particularly anointed time, and he will attack. Fear is one way he attacks, because he knows that fear is a faith destroyer.

Chapter Six

Forget the Failures

As you begin healing the sick and expecting signs, wonders, and miracles, don't let a failure deter you. We all have failures. Failure will happen; it's a part of growing in the ministry of healing and miracles. Just forget about the failures, and go on to the next person who needs healing. Even Paul faced failures. He had to leave a member of his team, Trophimus, sick in Miletus (2 Timothy 4:20). I am certain that not only did Paul pray for him, but likely the other team members also prayed for the healing of Trophimus—yet he remained ill.

Another member of Paul's team, Epaphroditus, was sick and almost died (Galatians 2:27). That doesn't sound like the beginning of a powerful healing ministry, does it?

Early in my ministry a young couple was told by someone that if they brought their sick baby to me that the baby would be healed. They brought the baby from many miles away. It was late at night when they arrived, and we prayed. I got word a couple days later that the baby died that next morning. I was devastated.

If you allow failure to stop you from praying for the sick, you will quit because you **will** experience failure. It's like riding a bicycle—if you ride often enough, you will have mishaps, especially as a beginner.

In my hometown of Port Chester, New York, there was a hill near where I lived. As a young boy I would watch the older boys ride down this hill, wishing that I had a bike so that I could do the same. One Christmas morning, there it was: a brand new, red Schwinn bicycle. I was excited and I took my bike out the front door and walked up the hill so that I could ride down it like the older boys did. I went to the top of the hill, got on my bike and down I went. The only problem was, I had never been on a bike before, and I didn't know how to steer it or stop it. I got about half-way down and veered off the road and crashed into the hedges in front of the Porter family house. I went flying over the hedges into their front yard. They were either going to church or coming from church, and there I was sprawled out in their front yard.

They asked, "Paul, are you okay?"

"Yeah, I'm okay." I said. I wasn't hurt, but I was really embarrassed.

I took my bike home so my dad could take the ruined front fender off. But I didn't quit riding my bike just because I had a mishap. In fact, I learned to ride really well, and fast.

Some time later, I was riding my bike really fast on the sidewalk not far from home, but I had to shoot out into the street because some women were walking on the sidewalk ahead of me. I jumped the curb and shot out into the road. I hit a car so hard on the rear quarter panel, that it fish-tailed (swerved), and I went flying over the car, landing in the street. I stayed in the hospital overnight for observation, but I was not hurt. Still I didn't quit riding my bike. You would think that maybe I would quit, but I loved riding my bike.

Another time after that incident, I had to take my tires to the bike shop for some repair work. As I was crossing the large square in my hometown carrying my tires, I walked out between two parked cars and was hit by a truck. A crowd gathered around me, and as I scrambled to my feet, I passed out, and the truck driver caught me just before I hit the ground. I got to my feet and the crowd was looking at me wondering if I was hurt, when this friend of mine came up to me carrying my tires, and said, "Paul, I found your tires, but I can't find the rest of your bike." The crowd, thinking that I was riding a bike, let out a loud groan. Once again, I had to stay in the hospital overnight for observation. (My poor mother!)

Healing the sick is a lot like riding a bike; if you fall, you must get up and go again.

Jesus couldn't do many miracles in his hometown because of the people's lack of faith; not even Jesus could overcome the lack of faith in the people:

> "Where did this man get this wisdom and these miraculous powers?" they asked.
>
> "Isn't this the carpenter's son? Isn't his mother's name Mary, and aren't his brothers James, Joseph, Simon and Judas? Aren't all his sisters with us? Where then did this man get all these things?"
>
> And they took offense at him. But Jesus said to them, "Only in his hometown and in his own house is a prophet without honor."
> And he did not do many miracles there because of their lack of faith.
>
> MATTHEW 13:55-58

They took offense at Jesus and would in no way honor him. People with an ordinary lack of faith can be healed and even do the healing;

beginners don't start with a great amount of faith, and yet they can heal the sick. I've seen this on many occasions where beginners with very little faith can be effective in healing the sick. Sometimes people have an extraordinary amount of unbelief because they have been taught against biblical healing as not being valid, or they resent the person doing the healing, or for some other extraordinary reason. In these cases, it will be difficult to see healing and miracles.

Jesus faced ridicule, and even had people laugh at Him, as in the case when he went to heal the synagogue ruler's daughter:

> *When they came to the home of the synagogue leader, Jesus saw a commotion, with people crying and wailing loudly. He went in and said to them, "Why all this commotion and wailing? The child is not dead but asleep."* **But they laughed at him.**
>
> MARK 5:38-40 *(Author Emphasis)*

On his way to heal the synagogue leader's daughter, Jesus wouldn't let anyone follow him except Peter, James, and John. He put those who laughed at him and were crying and wailing loudly, out of the room. He allowed only Peter, James, John, and the parents of the girl to be with him as he healed the girl. He got rid of all those who were wallowing in unbelief, and only allowed only those with faith to be with him.

An ordinary lack of faith because of a lack of experience can be overcome, but sometimes failure occurs in a climate of extraordinary unbelief. No matter what you encounter, try to create an environment of faith. This is what Jesus did when he only allowed certain disciples and parents to follow him, and excluded those who were crying, wailing, and laughing at him.

Another time Jesus was wary of the climate of unbelief was in the city Bethsaida—a town notorious for its unbelief, (Matthew 11:21). This is the reason when a blind man was brought to Jesus, he immediately took the man outside the village of Bethsaida to heal him, and when the man was healed, Jesus sent him home, saying, "Don't even go into the village" (Mark 8:26). Jesus told him not to go through Bethsaida on his way home so he wouldn't lose his healing because of the influence of unbelief in that city.

Some Don't Want to be Healed

It is hard to fathom, but a sad fact is that some people with serious health problems don't want to be healed. In John 5 there is a story about a man who didn't want to be healed:

> *Now there is in Jerusalem near the Sheep Gate a pool, which in Aramaic is called Bethesda and which is surrounded by five covered colonnades. Here a great number of disabled people gathered—the blind, the lame, paralyzed, etc. One who was there had been an invalid for thirty-eight years. When Jesus saw him lying there and learned that he had been in this condition for a long time, he asked him, "Do you want to get well?"*
>
> *"Sir," the invalid replied, "I have no one to help me into the pool when the water is stirred. While I am trying to get in, someone else goes down ahead of me."*
>
> *Then Jesus said to him, "Get up! Pick up your mat and walk."*
>
> *At once the man was cured; he picked up his mat and walked.*
>
> JOHN 5:2-9

This man had been an invalid for thirty-eight years, and probably spent much of that time at the pool enjoying the fellowship of the other folks in sickbay. His excuse was that when the water was stirred there was nobody to help him get in it. I would have to say that in all those thirty-eight years, he surely should have figured out how to get in the pool and get his healing. He enjoyed lying around at poolside, and having fellowship with the other paralytics, blind, and lame people. He had been doing this for a long time and enjoyed it; he was satisfied with not being healed.

The man had a poor excuse for not being healed, but in spite of his excuse, Jesus healed him anyway. When someone is healed it changes their life. It elevates their faith, and causes them to trust God, but they also have to go get a job and go to work. Some people don't want to do that; they would rather stay poolside and collect benefits.

> WHEN SOMEONE IS HEALED IT CHANGES THEIR LIFE

The lame beggar, who was healed by Peter and John at the Gate Beautiful (Acts 3), had been born crippled and had never worked a day in his life. The only job he had ever known was begging. After he was healed he was walking, and leaping, and praising God, but when things settled down, he had to deal with his new life. He couldn't beg anymore. He had to deal with earning a living in some other way—he had to get a job. We sometimes forget to think about the differences it makes in a person's life, and the changes the person will have to deal with. He had no experience with working, no training, no resume, and perhaps no desire, but he knew that he wanted to be healed.

I have actually had several people say that they wanted a particular body part healed, but they didn't want a total healing because if they did they would lose their disability pension.

Some can't be healed because of a hardness of heart toward God, arrogance against God, or an unwillingness to repent, as was the case of Herod in the book of Acts. Sitting on a throne and wearing his royal robes, Herod gave a public address to the people of Tyre and Sidon, and when he was done they shouted, "This is the voice of a god, not of a man" (Acts 12:22). Because he didn't give praise to God, he was struck down and eaten by worms and died. He couldn't be healed because of his arrogance, and at that moment the parasites within him feasted.

We never want to cast our pearls before swine, but sometimes it is hard to discern the fine line between the swine and the ignorant.

The Pharisees couldn't be healed because they were hypocrites (swine), and even though they saw the miracles they would not believe:

Even after Jesus had performed so many signs in their presence, they still would not believe in him. This was to fulfill the word of Isaiah the prophet:

"Lord, who has believed our message and to whom has the arm of the Lord been revealed?"

For this reason they could not believe, because, as Isaiah says elsewhere:

"He has blinded their eyes and hardened their hearts, so they can neither see with their eyes, nor understand with their hearts, nor turn—and I would heal them."

Isaiah said this because he saw Jesus' glory and spoke about him.

> "Lord, who has believed our message and to whom has the arm of the Lord been revealed?"
>
> JOHN 12:38-41

> Many even among the leaders did believe in Jesus. But **because of fear for their religious position** they would not openly acknowledge their faith, for fear they would be put out of the synagogue; for **they loved human praise more than praise from God.**
>
> JOHN 11:37-42 *(Author Emphasis)*

In Athens, Paul didn't do any miracles (Acts 17:16) because the Athenians just wanted to hear the latest news, ideas, theories, and gossip so they could talk about it. They probably would have treated the miracles of God as pearls to be trampled on in their debating forums. Consequently, there were not any conversions, because the basic strategy that Jesus gave us was not utilized. Paul did not do any miracles, consequently, he did not have much success in Athens.

Jesus was very critical of the generation of people of His day. Speaking of that generation he said:

> *To what can I compare this generation? They are like children sitting in the marketplaces and calling out to others: "We played the pipe for you, and you did not dance; we sang a dirge, and you did not mourn."*
>
> MATTHEW 11:16-17

What Jesus meant was that he tried everything to get them to respond to the call of God, but they wouldn't. If he played the flute they would not dance and celebrate, and if he played a funeral dirge they would ignore the time for mourning. They would do their own thing, no matter what, in rebellion toward God.

Jesus began his ministry in a dead generation, which was getting worse until it ended in 70 A.D. (a religion that was led by Pharisees and Sadducees), its nation destroyed, and its people either killed or dispersed. Jesus said that it was an "unbelieving and perverse generation" (Matt 14:17).

Some don't want to be healed by God because they didn't want God. This is difficult to believe, but never-the-less true.

ISSUES TO DEAL WITH

The Holy Spirit won't (normally) heal where there is no faith. The Holy Spirit would like to heal people, and wants to heal people, but he won't go against the will of the people. Not even the creator will overcome someone's resistance to the Gospel.

Seeing miracles can cause people to repent most of the time, but not always. The people of Chorazin and Bethsaida did not repent even though they witnessed miracles:

> *Woe to you, Chorazin! Woe to you, Bethsaida! For if the miracles that were performed in you had been performed in Tyre and Sidon, they would have repented long ago in sackcloth and ashes.*
>
> MATTHEW 11:21

The disciples had amazing results, as recorded in the book of Acts:

> *Crowds gathered also from the towns around Jerusalem, bringing their sick and those tormented by impure spirits, and all of them were healed.*
>
> ACTS 5:16

In view of all of them being healed, why is it that today we often see that some are not healed? When someone is not healed, oftentimes we don't have any idea why. Even the Apostle Paul had an ailment that he mentions:

As you know, it was because of an illness that I first preached the Gospel to you. Even though my illness was a trial to you, you did not treat me with contempt or scorn.

GALATIANS 4:13-14

It is obvious then that even godly people sometimes get sick and not have an immediate healing. There are some obvious reasons why some are not healed, and I would like to offer a few:

- Embracing a theology that says that healing is not for today
- Lack of faith
- Double mindedness
- Inappropriate dealing with the Body of Christ
- Unforgiveness
- Lack of repentance

Some are not healed because of sin. I'm not saying that sin is the cause of all sickness, but I am saying that if there is unrepentant sin it could prevent a healing.

As in the two following examples, sin will sometimes (1) be the cause of sickness, and sometimes (2) it is not caused from sin, but the healing is to bring glory to God.

1. In 1 Corinthians 11:27-30 we can see that **there is a definite connection between sin and sickness:**

Whoever eats the bread or drinks the cup of the Lord in an unworthy manner will be guilty of sinning against the body and blood of the Lord. A man ought to examine himself before he eats of the bread and drinks of the cup. For anyone who eats and drinks without recognizing the body of the Lord eats and drinks judgment on himself. That is why many among you are weak and sick, and a number of you have fallen asleep.

So it is abundantly clear that sin, in this instance, causes sickness and even death.

2. However, in the following Scripture, **it is clear that in this case, sin did not cause sickness.** Jesus is asked if a blind person's condition was caused by sin.

As he went along, he saw a man blind from birth. His disciples asked him, "Rabbi, who sinned, this man or his parents, that he was born blind?"
"Neither this man nor his parents sinned," said Jesus, "but this happened so that the work of God might be displayed in his life."

JOHN 9:1-3

Although **sin can sometimes cause sickness**, and prevent someone from being healed, **sin is not always the cause of sickness**:

Because of your wrath there is no health in my body; there is no soundness in my bones because of my sin.

PSALM 28:2

When I kept silent, my bones wasted away through my groaning all day long. For day and night your hand was heavy on me; my strength was sapped as in the heat of summer. Then I acknowledged my sin to you and did not cover up my iniquity. I said, "I will confess my transgressions to the LORD." And you forgave the guilt of my sin.

PSALM 32:3-5

This Scripture makes it clear that sin must be dealt with before healing: If they have sinned, they will be forgiven.

> *Later Jesus found him at the temple and said to him, "See, you are well again. Stop sinning or something worse may happen to you."*
>
> JOHN 5:14

The good news is that we can repent and move on with God. Many Christians don't need to repent prior to healing the sick, because they live a life of repentance. Just to make sure, it is best to repent, whether you need a healing or are praying for the sick. Sin must be dealt with in the fundamental shift of repentance, and it will clear the way for a divine flow of the Holy Spirit. Repentance not only wipes out sin, but it refreshes:

> *Repent, then, and turn to God, so that your sins may be wiped out, that times of refreshing may come from the Lord.*
>
> ACTS 3:19

Repentance is clearing the deck for the cleansing of sin. It loosens every demonic stronghold and all sickness and disease.

> *Some became fools through their rebellious ways and suffered affliction because of their iniquities. They loathed all food and drew near the gates of death. Then they cried to the LORD in their trouble, and he saved them from their distress. He sent out his word and healed them.*
>
> PSALM 107:17-20

CHAPTER SEVEN

Deliverance and Healing

As we search the Scriptures, we find that healing and deliverance are dealt with in a similar manner; there are no exceptions to this. All healing and deliverance is done with a simple word (or words) of authority. The only difference would be the changing of a few words. As an example, instead of saying, "in Jesus' name be healed," we might say, "In Jesus' name come out of him (or her), you evil spirit." The word of authority is always directed toward a singular entity. Jesus said that we could speak to the mountain and it would be cast into the sea.

An interesting question to ask is this: is this sickness caused by a demon or does it have a natural cause? We don't always know; consequently, they would be ministered to in the same manner. That is what Jesus did; he treated all healing in the same manner—with words of authority. He used different wording according to the situation, but it was always a word of authority.

In Mark 5 Jesus said to the demoniac, "Come out of this man, you impure spirit!" However, when he healed the woman who was crippled by an evil spirit for eighteen years, he said, "Woman, you are set free from your infirmity." And with those simple words of authority, she was delivered from an evil spirit and consequently healed.

Whether we like it or not we have to deal with demons; they are our enemy. Casting out a demon (what some would call exorcism or deliverance which is nothing more than driving out evil spirits from a person) sounds like a very ominous thing to be involved in, but that is not the case. In fact, it is very common. Although it is not talked about in public, there are multiple thousands of people who administer deliverance in the United States alone. It is common among Pentecostal, Charismatic, and evangelical churches—often carried out by young Christians.

The Apostle John saw a stranger driving out demons and told Jesus about it. Jesus said that they were doing a miracle:

> "Teacher," said John, "we saw a man driving out demons in your name and we told him to stop, because he was not one of us."
> "Do not stop him," Jesus said. "No one who does a miracle in my name can in the next moment say anything bad about me."
>
> MARK 9:38-39

Jesus said that driving out a demon is a miracle, and if it is a miracle, we should want to participate. Also, when a demon is driven out of a person, that person has the Kingdom come on them:

> *If I drive out demons by the Spirit of God, then the Kingdom of God has come upon you.*
>
> MATTHEW 12:28

According to Scripture, if a person has a demon cast out of them, they've experienced a miracle. They had the Kingdom come upon them, and they were healed in the process. It is impossible to look at this subject in Scripture and not realize that we are supposed to confront the enemy.

All the battles of the Old Testament are a type and shadow of the battles going on today with the unseen demonic/satanic world. That is why the Father would often tell the army of Israel to destroy everything that belonged to the opposing army, just as Jesus came to destroy the work of the devil in its entirety.

When we study the Scriptures, we see that it is impossible to separate deliverance from healing. Jesus mentions both healing and deliverance in the same breath, in the same paragraph, and in the same context:

As you go, preach this message: "The Kingdom of Heaven is near. Heal the sick, raise the dead, cleanse those who have leprosy, drive out demons."

MATTHEW 10:7

Driving out demons produces healing, so, it is impossible to separate deliverance (casting out demons) from healing. In fact, deliverance is the same as healing because that is what it produces.

It is impossible to prove conclusively that every sickness is caused by a demon. However, the Bible does indicate the relationship between healing and deliverance. Peter said:

How God anointed Jesus of Nazareth with the Holy Spirit and power, and how he went around doing good and healing all who were under the power of the devil, because God was with him.

ACTS 10:30

Jesus healed all who were under the power of the devil; this indicates that deliverance produces healing.

Let's look at some other Scriptures that indicate that deliverance results in healing:

> *When evening came, many who were demon-possessed were brought to him, and he drove out the spirits with a word and healed all the sick. This was to fulfill what was spoken through the prophet Isaiah: "He took up our infirmities and carried our diseases."*
>
> MATTHEW 8:16-17

> *On a Sabbath Jesus was teaching in one of the synagogues, and a woman was there who had been **crippled by a spirit for eighteen years.** She was bent over and could not straighten up at all. When Jesus saw her, he called her forward and said to her, "Woman, you are set free from your infirmity."*
>
> *Then he put His hands on her, and immediately she straightened up and praised God.*
>
> LUKE 13:10-13 (Author Emphasis)

> *A man in the crowd answered, "Teacher, I brought you my son, who is **possessed by a spirit that has robbed him of speech."***
>
> MARK 9:17-29 (Author Emphasis)

> *When they came to the crowd, a man approached Jesus and knelt before Him. "Lord, have mercy on my son," he said. "He has seizures and is suffering greatly. He often falls into the fire or into the water."*
>
> *… Jesus rebuked the demon, and it came out of the boy, and he was healed from that moment.*
>
> MATTHEW 17:14-20

Crowds gathered also from the towns around Jerusalem, **bringing their sick and those tormented by impure spirits, and all of them were healed.**

ACTS 5:16 *(Author Emphasis)*

In many instances in the New Testament, healing and deliverance are mentioned together, which reinforces the fact that they are inseparable. When one speaks of healing, it must include deliverance (driving out demons). The Scriptures are pretty clear that they both produce healing, and they are certainly integrated, but there is a blurred line about whether all healing is demonic.

Now, the question we must ask is this: Does the New Testament say that there are any infirmities, sickness, diseases, which have their origin in a natural cause of any kind? No! But there is overwhelming evidence of infirmities, diseases, and sicknesses caused by evil spirits! In fact, it is overwhelming that infirmities, diseases, and sicknesses are caused by evil spirits rather than by a natural cause.

> THERE IS OVERWHELMING EVIDENCE OF SICKNESS CAUSED BY EVIL SPIRITS

I first saw the connection between healing and deliverance when a man in the church I pastored had a massive heart attack. He had blown out all the main arteries in his heart, and the family was told that they should make out his will because there was nothing the doctors or the hospital could do for him except make him as comfortable as possible, while he was dying.

It was seven days before I heard about his condition, and went to the hospital to see him. He was seated on the edge of the bed; he was in too much pain to lie down, and didn't have enough strength to stand. He was horribly bloated, and could barely utter a few words, and had not eaten or gone to the bathroom in seven days.

I was sitting there looking at him when the Holy Spirit said to me, "Come against the spirit of death." I can't say that I rose up in faith, or felt anything. I simply said, "In Jesus' name, I come against the spirit of death, and command it to leave." I think that was all that I said. It was less than a minute when he began to stir; then he stood and walked to the bathroom, and I could hear him using the urinal. When he came out he walked out in the hallway and asked the nurse if he could get something to eat. When he came back into the room, it was then that it hit both of us that God had healed him, completely and instantaneously.

He was kept in the hospital for three more days, and each day they would take him before a panel of ten or twelve medical doctors and psychiatrists to question him about his healing. And each day he gave the same answer, "My pastor came here and prayed for me and God healed me." The medical people were not satisfied with that answer, and insisted he give them a rational explanation, but he had nothing rational to give them.

This incident happened many years ago, but it was the first time that I saw the relationship between healing and driving out an evil spirit; a simple word of authority was all that was necessary

> *When Jesus' disciples asked him why they couldn't heal the boy from seizures, Jesus didn't give some long explanation on the difference between deliverance and healing. He just said, "For truly, I say to you, if you have faith like a grain of mustard seed, you will **say to this mountain, 'Move from here to there,' and it will move, and nothing will be impossible for you.**"*
>
> MATTHEW 17:19-20 *(Author Emphasis)*

This is the basis that we should use for healing the sick. We should approach it like it is some mountain (obstacle) that has to be removed. When ministering healing in a group or in front of a crowd, if you are speaking to the mountains in someone's life, only the most discerning will ever be aware that demons are being driven out.

I was at an institution for the mentally challenged some years ago, and I was in an open ward with the most difficult cases. I was there because I wanted to pray for a particular person, but I couldn't get near him. While I was waiting patiently for an opportunity, I noticed a patient that was pacing quickly around the large room, and when a commercial would come on the TV, he would stand in front of the set and mimic it. He walked by me several times, and as he went by he would extend his left hand, and shake my hand. A nurse told me that this man could not speak a word of English. But as I was about to leave, he came up to me and pointed to the Bible that I was carrying under my arm, and asked me in perfect English, "What is that?" I said, "It's my Bible."

Again, he spoke in perfect English, and said, "Genesis 6:11." I quickly opened my Bible to Genesis 6:11 and read, "The earth was corrupt in God's sight and was full of violence."

Demons know what is going on, they are not stupid, but they have no defense against the Christian that is removing mountains.

If you are regularly healing the sick, the demons know who you are. That is why when you minister to a person a second time, it will be easier because the demons recognize the authority that you carry. They will begin to manifest and even leave before you start to pray. They will begin leaving (sometimes) before you say a word because they know who you are.

Deliverance, the First Time

Many years ago as a young Christian, I was having a conversation with a man who was telling me about all the physical and mental problems he was having. He went on and on about all his problems, and while he was speaking I heard myself saying, "You need deliverance." I wondered to myself, "Why did I say that?"

He agreed with me, and kept on talking about his problems. I then heard myself saying, "Do you want me to minister deliverance to you?"

Again I wondered why I said that; I had never ministered deliverance, and didn't know anything about it. He said that he did, and I agreed that in three days we would get together. I needed that time to figure out what I was going to do! Frankly, I didn't have the faintest idea, but I knew that the Holy Spirit was directing me to do something.

I tried to find some reading material on deliverance, but couldn't. I decided that the best thing I could do was to use the portion of Scripture in Mark 5:1-13 as my model where Jesus confronted the Gadarene demoniac and asked him to identify himself, by asking him, "What is your name?"

The demoniac replied by saying, "My name is Legion." Then Jesus sent the demons into a herd of pigs, and they rushed down a steep bank into the lake and drowned.

I wanted to keep it as simple as possible, so I broke it down to these very simple components:

- Ask the demon his name.
- Get a reply from the demon.
- Drive the demon out.

I didn't have any pigs at hand, so I couldn't tell them to go into pigs. I figured that they could go where they wanted to go. But I did know the Bible says that they would go to dry places. I figured wherever those dry places were, that's where they would go:

> *When an impure spirit comes out of a person, it goes through arid places seeking rest and does not find it.*
>
> LUKE 11:24

When we met three days later, I didn't let on that I didn't know what I was doing. I thought if he knew it was my first time, it would make him uncomfortable (to say the least). I asked a faithful friend, Tom Posillipo, to join me, but I didn't tell him either. I was going to pretend to know what I was doing with both of them, so they wouldn't be fearful.

I started out by praying a prayer that I thought was appropriate. I tried to act full of faith and confidence, and I started the deliverance by asking, "What is your name?" This is what Jesus did so I assumed this would be a good place to start. I repeated that question ("Evil spirit, what is your name?") about ten times, and nothing happened. At this point I wanted to go hide under a rock or go home; I certainly didn't want to be there. I felt like a total idiot, but on the eleventh try, something happened. The demon spoke through the young man and said, "My name is Fear." I was really excited, but I didn't let him know it. I just pretended that it was business as usual.

Then I said the next thing that I thought was appropriate, "In Jesus' name, I command you to leave." But nothing happened.

Having no other brilliant ideas, I repeated that phrase about ten more times. Just about the time I was ready to quit, the young man erupted and threw up in the nearby sink, and the spirit of fear had gone. Again, I was excited.

I repeated the same scenario, asking for other names and repeating the same technique until we thought we had the demons all driven out—but we didn't. I did what so many do. It's a classic mistake, which produces many manifestations, but frankly, it doesn't produce much fruit.

IT'S AS SIMPLE AS FOLLOWING THE MODEL

When I began doing deliverance there was a widely held belief that a Christian couldn't be demonized. They could have sin or cancer or arthritis or diabetes … but they couldn't have a demon. Even though the majority of Christians at this time didn't believe in deliverance for Christians, I knew it was so, because I experienced it. Consequently, I was able to see it clearly in the Scriptures.

The vast majority of healing in the New Testament was from driving out demons. All that is necessary to be successful is to follow the model displayed in the New Testament. The seventy-two that were sent out were all novices, and they came back saying that even the demons submitted to them. Even though they were all novices, they had immediate success because they followed the model of Jesus' ministry.

There was a man in the New Testament driving out demons, and the disciples were upset because they did not recognize him:

> *"Teacher," said John, "we saw someone driving out demons in your name and we told him to stop, because he was not one of us."*
> *"Do not stop him," Jesus said. "For no one who does a miracle in my name can in the next moment say anything bad about me."*
>
> MARK 9:38-39

If novices with no theological background, special training, or spiritual mentoring can cast out demons, it can't be that difficult. By following the model they observed in Jesus, they were able to do it effortlessly.

One of the common mistakes made by many who administer deliverance is in an area known as "demonology." They try to name demons for everything, and have names for every manifestation of the sickness. This is a ruse of the enemy that will allow you to see manifestations, but never see a full, complete healing. They will have you running around trying to figure out the next move, or the next demon to name, when it is totally unnecessary. It is only necessary to go after the mountain—and all the trees, shrubs, rocks, grass, everything that is part of the mountain will follow! We don't even have to know the name of the mountain; we can do what Jesus and his disciples did: call it an evil spirit, and speak a word of authority.

Many ministers who study demonology and use it while doing deliverance will admit (when pressed) that although that they see incredible manifestations, they rarely see the desired healing.

Some of that error is from a poor understanding of the Mark 5:1-13 account of the demoniac from the Gadarenes. This is what I did in the account of the first time doing deliverance. I started by wanting the name of the demons because I misunderstood what Jesus did. Jesus never used the name "Legion," which is how the demon identified himself. The first thing that Jesus said to the demoniac was "Come out of this man, you impure spirit!" Then the demon asked permission to go into the pigs, and in response to that, Jesus said "go" (Matthew 8:32). Although, Jesus asked him his name, Jesus never repeated the name Legion in driving the demon into the pigs. Jesus said only three things (he also answered, "Go," when he allowed the demons to go into the pigs). He definitely never repeated the name Legion, and he never used a plural term in dealing with Legion. He just dealt with the mountain. Jesus simply removed the mountain, as he taught his disciples to do.

> *If you have faith as small as a mustard seed, you can say to this mountain, "Move from here to there," and it will move.*
>
> MATTHEW 17:20

Mountain is singular, and so was the phrase Jesus used in driving out the demons from the demoniac. He said, "Come out of this man, you impure spirit!" Jesus used this singular phrase, even though the demon said that there were many demons in the man: "My name is Legion," he replied, "for we are many."

> *The impure spirits came out and went into the pigs. The herd, about two thousand in number, rushed down the steep bank into the lake and were drowned.*
>
> MARK 5:13

Using "mountain" as a metaphor, notice that Jesus didn't try to drive out the trees, dirt, and rocks that comprised the mountain. Instead he did exactly what he taught his disciples: when he removed the mountain, the whole mountain (including, trees, dirt, and rocks) went into the pigs.

If we use Jesus' model, we will go after the mountain using a singular term and not get bogged down trying to name each rock and stone and removing them individually.

If you focus your attention and energy on all the things which comprise the mountain—naming each demons and all the various names of sickness, then you often miss the mountain all together. This was never done in the New Testament, since in the New Testament we are operating under new rules of having authority over all the power of the enemy.

Allow me a moment of redundancy while I repeat some of the material found elsewhere in this manuscript. It is necessary for me to do this in order to give a scenario of how a deliverance (or healing) works.

We utilize three components, faith, power, and authority.

The spirit-filled Christian has three biblical components when ministering healing or deliverance:

- faith (in Jesus),
- power (the Holy Spirit),
- and authority (the Father).

When we pray for the sick, these components are the basis by which we can heal the sick and drive out demons.

We also utilize these three aggressive components: using the name of Jesus, speaking to the mountain, and the laying on of hands.

When we engage the person who needs healing and deliverance, we do so using these three biblical components.

We use the name of Jesus whenever we do deliverance or heal the sick; that's primary. Then we speak to the issue, or we lay on hands, or we do both.

We utilize the finger of God, which is Jesus, the Holy Spirit, and the Father, working with us.

The reason we only have to speak to a single entity (the mountain) is that all healing is done by the finger of God. When the finger of God (Holy Spirit) is engaged (Luke 11:20), he is the one who figures things out. He removes the mountain and all the trees, shrubs, grass, and rocks, (demons). When we allow him to do it, it is then done efficiently and effectively. When we try to figure this out, we attempt to deal with each tree, shrub, or rock and never effectively move the mountain.

The finger of God will work on our behalf, automatically driving out the entities that he deems necessary to be driven out. We simply speak to the mountain and let the finger of God drive the mountain into the sea.

The following is an example of the finger of God driving out the enemy, in the proper sequence, as only he can do.

> *The Lord your God will drive out those nations before you, little by little. You will not be allowed to eliminate them all at once, or the wild animals will multiply around you. But the Lord your God will deliver them over to you, throwing them into great confusion until they are destroyed.*
>
> DEUTERONOMY 7:22-23

Mark 16:20 says that Jesus will work with us in signs, in order to confirm his Word. The Father, Son, and Holy Spirit work with us, and it is they who sort things out, drive out what needs to go, and determine the sequence in which it needs to go.

Deliverance is so simple that even novices are incredibly effective when using the biblical model. This is why the seventy-two novices in Luke 10:1 and the stranger in Mark 9:38-39 were effectively able drive out demons.

Pay attention to how Jesus drove out demons:

> *Many who were demon-possessed were brought to him, and he drove out the spirits with a word and healed all the sick.*
>
> MATTHEW 8:16

Jesus drove out evil spirits with a word and so did the disciples. Jesus and his disciples didn't go through all the sorts of unbiblical gyrations.

Pick a Fight

We can use subtle weapons against the enemy (unity and servanthood, etc.), but I think we should also just outright go ahead and pick a fight with him. Elijah picked a fight with Ahab, and every false religious leader in Israel when he said:

> *Summon the people from all over Israel to meet me on Mount Carmel. And bring the four hundred and fifty prophets of Baal and the four hundred prophets of Asherah, who eat at Jezebel's table.*
>
> 1 Kings 18:19

> *Elijah told the people to get two bulls, one for him and one for the prophets of Baal. Then put wood on and around the bull and light it on fire. Then the prophets of Ball are to call on the name of their god, and Elijah will call on the name of the Lord, and "the god who answers by fire—he is God."*
>
> 1 Kings 18:23-24

> *Then they (Baal's prophets) called on the name of Baal from morning till noon. "Baal, answer us!" they shouted. But there was no response; no one answered.*

> *And they danced around the altar they had made. At noon Elijah began to taunt them. "Shout louder!" he said. "Surely he is a god! Perhaps he is deep in thought, or busy, or traveling. Maybe he is sleeping and must be awakened."*

> *So they shouted louder and slashed themselves with swords and spears, as was their custom, until their blood flowed. Midday passed, and they continued their frantic prophesying until the time for the evening sacrifice. But there was no response, no one answered, no one paid attention.*
>
> 1 KINGS 18:26-29

After all the shouting and antics of the prophets of Baal, Elijah said:

> *"Answer me, Lord, answer me, so these people will know that you, Lord, are God, and that you are turning their hearts back again." Then the fire of the Lord fell and burned up the sacrifice, the wood, the stones and the soil, and also licked up the water in the trench. When all the people saw this, they fell prostrate and cried, "The Lord—he is God! The Lord—he is God!"*
>
> 1 KINGS 18:37-39

Elijah picked that fight to demonstrate to all Israel who the real God was, and he did it in convincing fashion because God had no real competitors to challenge him. There was a willingness on God's part to use his people to demonstrate his power, so that all will know there is none other. So let's go ahead and pick a fight, since we have superior power and authority.

The Apostle Paul offered a similar challenge as Elijah did:

> *I will come to you very soon, if the Lord is willing, and then I will find out not only how these arrogant people are talking, but what power they have. For the kingdom of God is not a matter of talk but of power.*
>
> 1 CORINTHIANS 4:19-20

I think it's our calling to pick a fight with the enemy.

Warning About Deliverance (Healing)

In Hollywood movies we see confrontation between people and demons where demons have so much power. This is because there aren't any real Christians in those movies. If there were, those movies would be boring, and very short—the demons would appear and the Christian would drive them out, and that would be the end of the movie.

A warning given to Christians about demons is when Jesus said, "Do not rejoice that the spirits submit to you, but rejoice that your names are written in Heaven" (Luke 10:18-20). Don't rejoice over having victory over demons, but rejoice over our salvation.

As a young Christian, I got into pride after casting out a demon. When I was just learning about it all, a man heard that I did deliverance, and asked me to minister to his son who was demonized. I agreed. Afterward I felt a sense of accomplishment and pride. It wasn't a particularly eventful time of ministry, but I was gloating over having power over the demons.

The next day I had to travel to another state to speak at a church, and when I got to my hotel room in that city, I opened my Bible and happened to read in Luke 12:10. *"Everyone who speaks a word against the Son of Man will be forgiven, but anyone who blasphemes against the Holy Spirit will not be forgiven."*

When I read those words, I totally believed that that is what I did, and suddenly I felt a tremendous heaviness on me. (There is no way that I can accurately describe what happened next). I believed that I had blasphemed the Holy Spirit, and I was going to hell.

I remember, vividly, walking around the motel room wondering what I could do, and I had no idea. God allowed me to feel what it was like being condemned to hell. I thought to myself, "I will serve God anyway," but I realized that in my present condition, I was incapable of functioning. The only thing that I could think of to do was to walk down the highway until I disintegrated. That was the only thing my clouded mind could think of because the only thing in my future was hell.

I walked by the large mirror in my motel room, and I would look in the mirror, and think, "You're nothing without Christ."

"I'm less than nothing without Jesus," I thought. "It would have been better that I were never born than to be without him."

The feeling was intense. It literally felt like I was weighted down by hundreds of pounds. My mind was clouded, and I felt totally alone and isolated from any help. After going through this for what felt like hours (though I don't know the actual amount of time), I had some relief, but then I would go back into it again. This went back and forth for a while, until, totally exhausted, I fell asleep.

The next morning I called a friend, an older believer, who assured me that it wasn't real, and I had not been condemned to hell. With that assurance, I began to feel better. However, when I gave my message at church that morning, I could still feel some of the effects of that traumatic night. My voice was halting and as I listened to the tape later, it sounded like I was under stress.

I believe that God allowed me to go through that experience to give me a valuable lesson: I am truly less than nothing without Jesus, and it would be better if I were never born than to not have a relationship with him. This understanding has served me well from that time until now. Christ in me is where all power lies.

Chapter Eight

The Enemy Wants You

The greatest contest of all contests is being played out—a contest that began in Heaven and has continued on earth. Lucifer (Satan) was thrown out of Heaven (Luke 10:18), and will eventually be crushed by the church (Romans 16:20).

We know what Satan's game plan is. We are not unaware of his schemes (2 Corinthians 2:11). The prophetic word from Ezekiel the prophet tells us:

> *By your wisdom and understanding you have gained wealth for yourself and amassed gold and silver in your treasuries. By your great skill in trading you have increased your wealth, and because of your wealth your heart has grown proud.*
>
> EZEKIEL 28:4-5

Satan is using wealth and the love of money on earth to draw people away from the living God. The "deceitfulness of wealth chokes the Word." So we must show people that there is a power beyond this world and greater than the allure of wealth.

When Jesus left the earth, he gave believers the responsibility of defeating Satan and his demons. We have authority to do it; we have the command to do it; and we have the prophetic word that it will be done:

> *The God of peace will soon crush Satan under your feet.*
>
> ROMANS 16:20

Many today don't or won't recognize the existence of the devil or demons, but the parable of the sower is an example of what they do when seed (the Word of God) is scattered along the path:

> *The devil comes and takes away the Word from their hearts, so that they may not believe and be saved.*
>
> LUKE 8:12

The devil steals the Word from people:

- to prevent them from being saved,
- to prevent them from being healed,
- to keep them from being set free from demons.

He is a subtle schemer, deceiver, murderer, and liar (John 8:44).

God Created the Devil

Since Jesus is the creator of all things, he created Satan and the demons as well:

> *The son is the image of the invisible God, the firstborn over all creation. For by Him all things were created: things in Heaven and on earth, visible and invisible, whether thrones or powers or rulers or*

authorities; all things were created by him and for him. He is before all things, and in him all things hold together.

COLOSSIANS 1:15-17

The false gods of this world and all enemies of God will fall before him, as in the case of Dagon, the false god of the Philistines:

After the Philistines had captured the ark of God, they took it from Ebenezer to Ashdod. Then they carried the ark into Dagon's temple and set it beside Dagon. When the people of Ashdod rose early the next day, there was Dagon, fallen on his face on the ground before the ark of the Lord!

They took Dagon and put him back in his place. But the following morning when they rose, there was Dagon, fallen on his face on the ground before the ark of the Lord! His head and hands had been broken off and were lying on the threshold; only his body remained. That is why to this day neither the priests of Dagon nor any others who enter Dagon's temple at Ashdod step on the threshold.

1 SAMUEL 5:1-5

God created Satan and his demons just for us, so that we could have an adversary. God uses Satan to perfect his saints, as in the case of the Apostle Paul when he said that he prayed to have a thorn in his flesh removed:

To keep me from becoming conceited because of the surpassing greatness of the revelations, a thorn was given me in the flesh, a messenger of Satan to harass me, to keep me from becoming conceited. Three times I pleaded with the Lord about this, that it should leave me. But he said to me, "My grace is sufficient for you, for my power is made perfect in weakness."

Therefore I will boast all the more gladly of my weaknesses, so that the power of Christ may rest upon me. For the sake of Christ, then, I am content with weaknesses, insults, hardships, persecutions, and calamities. For when I am weak, then I am strong.

2 Corinthians 12:7-9

Satan was sent to harass Paul, but the result was that Paul was strengthened in the things of God. He said, *"I will boast all the more gladly of my weaknesses, so that the power of Christ may rest upon me."*

Satan is used as a pawn by God to strengthen Christians (if we respond properly), as in the case of Paul who, through weakness, was strengthened.

God also uses Satan and his demons as agents of punishment against the wicked and unrighteous, and refers to the demons that do his bidding, as his fishermen and hunters. They do the Lord's bidding in the sense that they will find the wicked and repay them double for their wickedness and sin:

"But now I will send for many fishermen," declares the Lord, "and they will catch them. After that I will send for many hunters, and they will hunt them down on every mountain and hill and from the crevices of the rocks. My eyes are on all their ways; they are not hidden from me, nor is their sin concealed from my eyes. I will repay them double for their wickedness and their sin, because they have defiled my land with the lifeless forms of their vile images and have filled my inheritance with their detestable idols."

Jeremiah 16:16-18

As a fisherman would catch fish with hooks and nets so do demons catch the wicked:

> *You have made people like the fish in the sea, like the sea creatures that have no ruler. The wicked foe pulls all of them up with hooks, he catches them in his net, he gathers them up in his dragnet; and so he rejoices and is glad. Therefore he sacrifices to his net and burns incense to his dragnet, for by his net he lives in luxury and enjoys the choicest food. Is he to keep on emptying his net, destroying nations without mercy?*
>
> HABAKKUK 1: 14-17

Satan and his demons were created to test the believer and to deal harshly with the unbeliever. God declares:

> *"I will no longer drive out before them any of the nations Joshua left when he died. I will use them to test Israel and see whether they will keep the way of the Lord and walk in it as their ancestors did." The Lord had allowed those nations to remain; he did not drive them out at once by giving them into the hands of Joshua.*
>
> JUDGES 2:21-23

Satan and his demons were created so the children of God would have an opponent that would provide a means of testing. He used the serpent to test Adam and Eve in the Garden, and he used Pharaoh to test Moses when he led Israel out of Egypt. Without an adversary, there would be no opposition to carrying out the will of God, and faith would not be required.

Yes, God created the devil and he has a role in God's plan, but understand that in the end we will crush Satan.

A New Teaching

During the time when Jesus was on earth, he established a change in spiritual authority. The people of Jesus' time knew about demons, and they knew that demons caused sickness and disease. Up until that time demons operated out in the open because there were no threats to their activity; that is, until Jesus began his ministry, and gave Christians authority over them.

> *When Jesus began his ministry, the people were all so amazed that they asked each other,* **"What is this? A new teaching**—*and with authority! He even gives orders to impure spirits and they obey him."*
>
> MARK 1:27 *(Author Emphasis)*

There are still hunters and fishermen on the earth (demons), but they now come under a new rule. This is when things changed for demons; they no longer had free reign in peoples' lives. They had to have another plan, so they began hiding and not revealing that they existed. If they operated in the open, they would be dealt with and defeated by warring Christians.

Today, if someone threw himself into fire or water (like the boy in Matthew 17:14, whose father came to Jesus and wanted Jesus to heal him), it would not be recognized as a demon. The diagnosis, according to modern medicine, would be that the boy was suicidal, and they would probably medicate him. Modern psychiatry would not diagnose people like this as having a demon.

Demons operated out in the open until Jesus came with a new teaching (Mark 1:27); consequently, the demons went into hiding, knowing if they were exposed, they would be defeated.

In Moses' day, he was given authority to perform signs, wonders, and miracles to release Israel from the bondage of Egypt. When Moses was in Midian living with his father-in-law, God visited him in the burning bush, and told Moses that he was sending him to Pharaoh to plunder the Egyptians (Exodus 3:22).

Just as Jesus gave the disciples the authority to trample on snakes and scorpions and to overcome all the power of the enemy, that nothing would harm them (Luke 10:19), the Lord also gave power to Moses to overcome all the power of the enemy. He told Moses:

> *When you return to Egypt, see that you perform before Pharaoh all the wonders I have given you the power to do.*
>
> EXODUS 4:21

The devil is a pawn in the battle that is taking place, just as Pharaoh was a pawn during the exodus of Israel from Egypt. The Lord said to Moses:

> *Go to Pharaoh, for **I have hardened his heart** and the hearts of his officials so that I may perform these signs of mine among them that you may tell your children and grandchildren how I dealt harshly with the Egyptians and how I performed my signs among them, and that you may **know that I am the Lord.***
>
> EXODUS 10:1-2 *(Author Emphasis)*

Yes, It took miracles for Israel to be released from Egypt. In the same way it will take miracles to do the work of God in these days. Only, in this day, it is not one man leading the charge, as Moses did. In addition to the mature believer there will also be novices in the Body of Christ, performing signs, wonders, and miracles, because we have all been commissioned, commanded, and empowered.

From the beginning of time, it has been a major issue that the devil is to be defeated. Scripture says:

The reason the Son of God appeared was to destroy the devil's work.

1 JOHN 3:8

God anointed Jesus of Nazareth with the Holy Spirit and power, and how he went around doing good and healing all who were under the power of the devil, because God was with Him.

ACTS 10: 38

Satan's defeat is already sealed (Romans 16:20).

We already know that Satan and his demons will be defeated, but an important question is this: how much of the trouble in this world is caused by demons? The Scripture tells us that the battle we fight is not against flesh and blood. We don't fight against the seen, visible world, but every battle is against the spirit world, Satan and demons:

For our struggle is not against flesh and blood, *but against the rulers, against the authorities, against the powers of this dark world and against the spiritual forces of evil in the heavenly realms.*

EPHESIANS 6:12 *(Author Emphasis)*

If we fight against flesh we will lose the battle because the battle is not against flesh and blood. Our battle is against an unseen world that manifests in what is seen, but to fight against what we see is foolhardy. The unseen world pulls the strings which causes all things.

The devil and his demons are the author of all or almost all (whichever you want to believe) disease, sickness, malady, accidents, and ailments. "The thief comes **only** to steal and kill and destroy" (John 10:10). The "only" thing the devil has in mind concerning the people of the earth is to steal from them, kill them, and to destroy them.

The devil has a lot of influence on earth. When he fell from Heaven, one-third of the angels fell with him. This means that he had a lot of influence when he was in Heaven, and he probably has at least that much influence on the earth. Because he has a lot of influence on earth, it will take the power of the Holy Spirit in signs, wonders, and miracles to break this influence. Jesus said:

> *"I am sending you out like sheep among wolves. Therefore, be as shrewd as shakes and as innocent as doves."*
>
> MATTHEW 10:16

We are being sent out like sheep, but we only appear to be harmless; in reality, we have authority over all the power of every wolf.

WEAPONS OF WARFARE

We don't always have to have a direct confrontation with demons for them to be driven out. Demons are driven out at times when we are not even aware of it—during times of praise and worship, times of prayer and intercession, walking through a supermarket, at work, or at school. All Christians have a level of authority that demons recognize.

When Peter walked through the streets, people were healed and evil spirits were driven out by his shadow. This was because he carried an authority against such things as disease and demons, and the authority he carried defeated all such things as he walked the streets:

Paul drove out evil spirits and healed people by using handkerchiefs and aprons that he had touched. He transferred his authority to these objects, and they healed the sick and drove out demons. What does this tell us? We don't necessarily have to have a direct confrontation to drive out demons.

Granted, Paul and Peter were super apostles, but if that could be done with Paul's handkerchiefs and aprons and Peter's shadow, the average Christian should be able to do that to some degree, because the average Christian has the same Holy Spirit power as Paul and Peter.

We can confront evil anywhere we recognize it; it won't necessarily be in a church setting. I don't know who said this, but someone once said, "Only when battles are fought, do we have victory."

> WE CAN CONFRONT EVIL ANYWHERE WE RECOGNIZE IT

It doesn't matter where we encounter the enemy; through the power of the Holy Spirit we will demolish him, in any battlefield and at any time.

In 1 Kings 20:13, Ben-Hadad king of Aram mustered his entire army. Accompanied by thirty-two kings he went up and besieged Samaria and attacked it. A prophet went to the king of Israel and said:

> *This is what the Lord says: "Do you see this vast army? I will give it into your hand today, and then you will know that I am the Lord."*
>
> 1 KINGS 20:13

Ben-Hadad, the king of Aram was so confident that when it was reported that men of Israel were advancing, the King said, *"If they have come out for peace, take them alive; if they have come out for war, take them alive."* Either way it will not be difficult to take them alive. However, Israel advanced and inflicted heavy losses on the Arameans.

The officials of the king of Aram advised him, "Their gods are gods of the hills. That is why they were too strong for us. But if we fight them on the plains, surely we will be stronger than they."

The next spring, the Arameans went to fight against Israel again. "The Israelites camped opposite them like two small flocks of goats, while the Arameans covered the countryside.

1 KINGS 20:27

Israel was completely outmatched, but it didn't matter, for God was fighting for them because he wanted all to know that he is the Lord.

The man of God came up and told the king of Israel, "This is what the Lord says: 'Because the Arameans think the Lord is a god of the hills and not a god of the valleys, I will deliver this vast army into your hands, and **you will know that I am the Lord.'"**

1 KINGS 20:28 (Author Emphasis)

Every gift in the Christian's arsenal is a weapon to be used against the enemy. For every trick and deception of the enemy we have a remedy. We are at war, and it's kingdom against kingdom; every Christian should be armed and ready for every trick and deception of the enemy. The devil is a taker and we will overcome by giving; the devil hates so we must overcome by loving; the devil brings sickness and we will overcome by healing.

Healing and miracles will destroy the stronghold of unbelief. When Jesus *"was in Jerusalem at the Passover feast, many people saw the* **miraculous signs he was doing and believed in his name**" (John 2:23, Author Emphasis).

People will believe when they hear the Word being preached, and see the miracles. Miracles are powerful in destroying the stronghold of unbelief and turning people from the power of Satan to the power of God.

In June 2007, in a bombing attempt at the Glasgow Airport carried out by Muslim doctors, someone associated with the doctors said, "Those who cure you will kill you." What the Bible says is quite different than that of the Muslims. According to the New Testament, those who cure you will also love you. Our weapons of warfare are quite different than the Muslims, and, in fact, all other religions.

When David faced Goliath in the valley of Elah, he had exactly what he needed, a smooth stone. Goliath is described as a champion who was nine feet tall with a bronze helmet, a coat of scale armor weighing five thousand shekels, bronze greaves on his legs, and a spear like a weaver's rod. It sounds like a total mismatch, but God gave David exactly what he needed. David went to a nearby stream and picked five smooth stones. As he ran quickly to meet the giant, he pulled one of the stones from his bag, put it in his sling, and killed the giant. When we have prepared ourselves for battle, God will provide the stone or whatever is needed to confront the enemy. It will always be a mismatch because of God in us.

Chapter Nine

Keep It Simple

We tend to complicate things when it comes to healing and deliverance. Jesus gave extraordinarily simple instructions to his disciples about healing the sick and casting out demons. However, there are many successful healing ministries in the Body of Christ who use complicated means in healing and deliverance. Their teaching material may even have some non-biblical material with complicated methods and techniques. For the person just starting out in healing and deliverance, there are simple instructions that the Lord Jesus gives, which allow us to begin with confidence.

Whether it's healing or driving out demons, these are the basic methods. In fact, there is no difference between healing and deliverance except for the way we phrase the words of authority that we speak. These are the three methods:

1. We have permission to use the name of Jesus:
"In my name they will drive out demons"

MARK 16:17. *(Author Emphasis)*

2. We are to speak to the mountain:

"If you have faith as small as a mustard seed, you can say to this mountain, 'Move from here to there,' and it will move. Nothing will be impossible for you"

MATTHEW 17:20.

3. We are to lay hands on the sick:

"they will place their hands on sick people, and they will get well"

MARK 16:18.

These are the three components of the New Testament healing and deliverance given to us by Jesus. It can't get any simpler than that; just place your hands on the sick, and speak a word of authority in Jesus' name. Nothing else is necessary. Of course, we can say more, and we can repeat the word of authority until we get results.

We use the term "praying for the sick," but it's these three methods that we are referring to, (1) using the name of Jesus, (2) speaking to the mountain, and (3) laying hands on the sick. Even in this manuscript I use the term praying for the sick, but praying is done in conjunction with a word of authority.

If healing were too complicated, it would eliminate the novice from healing the sick. Healing the sick would be only for the elite who had a total grasp of the Scriptures along with all the methods and techniques. But healing is for everyone—the young Christians as well as the grounded and mature. There is no need for a great deal of sophistication or knowledge and extra-biblical and complicated teachings. Some study demonology in order to do deliverance, which is totally unnecessary. We are already aware of the devil's schemes, and we have authority over his power.

As we study the Scriptures we easily recognize that Jesus kept things simple, and keeping it simple goes to the root of his ministry. Many people think that healing is complicated; the story of Naaman is typical of that. When a servant girl heard about Naaman's leprosy, she informed him that he should go see the prophet. So he did. He went to see Elijah with his horses and chariots and stopped at the door of his house. Elijah didn't even come outside to see him, but instead sent him a message to go wash in the Jordan seven times and be healed (2 Kings 5:1-14).

Angry, Naaman went off in a rage. He had expected the prophet to come greet him, call on the name of the Lord, wave his hands over him and cure him. He almost missed out because the instruction was so simple it was insulting. Naaman's servants asked him if he would have done some great thing if the prophet had asked him to (2 Kings 5:13). He would have preferred a complicated, noble or difficult task of some kind.

Instead, he was being required to obey the Spirit of God. When he finally realized this, he went to the Jordan and did just as the prophet said and he "became clean like that of a young boy" (2 Kings 5:14). The leprosy was healed.

Jesus wasted neither energy nor words. He always spoke directly to the situation, sometimes with just a word or just by the laying on of his hands. He would speak a word filled with authority, and power. He likely never raised his voice above normal speaking tones. His ministry on earth was a great example of simplicity.

Here is a partial list of the words of authority Jesus and the disciples used:

- *"Be clean;"* Jesus said this to a man with leprosy (Matthew 8:3).

- *"He drove out the spirits with a word"* (Matthew 8:16).
- *"Get up, take up your mat and go home"* (Matthew 9:6).
- *"Stretch out your hand"* (Matthew 12:13).
- *"Jesus rebuked the demon"* (Matthew 17:18).
- *"Come out of him"* (Mark 1:25).
- *"Come out of this man, you evil spirit"* (Mark 5:8).
- *"Little girl, I say to you, get up"* (Mark 5:41).
- *"Be opened"* (Mark 7:34).
- *"I command you to come out of him and never enter him again"* Mark 9:25).
- *"He bent over and rebuked the fever"* Luke (4:39).
- *"Young man, I say to you, get up!"* (Luke 7:14).
- *"My child, get up!"* (Luke 8:54).
- *"Woman, you are set free from your infirmity"* (Luke 13:12).
- *"Get up, pick up your mat and walk"* (John 5:8).
- *"Go, wash in the pool of Siloam"* (John 9:7).
- *"Lazarus, come out"* (John 11:43).

The disciples followed the model they learned from Jesus.

- *"In the name of Jesus Christ of Nazareth, walk"* (Acts 3:6).
- *"Jesus Christ heals you. Get up and take care of your mat"* (Acts 9:32).

- *"Tabitha, get up"* (Acts 9:40).

- *"Stand up on your feet"* (Acts 14:10).

- *"In the name of Jesus Christ I command you to come out of her"* (Acts 16:18).

Besides using a word of authority, Jesus used a variety of ways to heal and deliver from evil spirits. Following is a partial list of the variety of ways that Jesus used:

- *"He touched her hand and the fever left her"* (Matthew 8:15).

- *"Touched their eyes"* (Matthew 20:34).

- *"All who touched him were healed"* (Mark 6:56).

- *"For such a reply you may go; the demon has left your daughter"* (Mark 7:29).

- *"Jesus put his hands on the man's eyes"* (Mark 8:25).

In the words of authority and the variety of ways Jesus used to heal and set people free from evil spirits, they all come down to the same three methods:

1. **In the name of Jesus**
2. **Speak to the mountain**
3. **The laying on of hands**

Many times they just touched his cloak, or he touched them, or he just told them that they were healed according to their faith.

We can also minister healing in the simplicity of the Word without complicated formulas. In fact, on a couple of occasions Jesus warned about saying too much (Matthew 5:34-37, Matthew 6:7-15). I'm not saying that too much verbiage is a bad thing, only that it isn't necessary. It is more important to say the right things and direct it accurately to have an effective, efficient, powerful healing ministry.

When Jesus encountered the fig tree in leaf that didn't have any fruit, in order to kill it for not bearing fruit, he simply said, *"May no one ever eat fruit from you again"* (Mark 11:14).

He didn't agonize over it with a long prayer, but spoke with an economy of words. His explanation to his disciples when Peter noticed the fig tree withered was "Have faith in God." Jesus answered:

> *Truly I tell you, if anyone says to this mountain, "Go, throw yourself into the sea," and does not doubt in their heart but believes that what they say will happen, it will be done for them.*
>
> MARK 11:22-23

We sometimes follow methods or traditions because it worked one time for someone else. We follow it because it had a dramatic impact, and seemed to be anointed.

I'm reminded of an illustration that someone once gave about Samson who, after striking down a thousand Philistines with the jawbone of an ass, threw away the jawbone never to use it again (Judges 15:17). We don't want to use jawbones that should have been discarded, but that is what we sometimes do when praying for the sick. We defer to the traditions of the church instead of the biblical model.

Jesus gives us some practical insights:

> *They came to Bethsaida, and some people brought a blind man and begged Jesus to touch Him. He took the blind man by the hand and led*

him outside the village. When he had spit on the man's eyes and put his hands on him, Jesus asked, "Do you see anything?"

He looked up and said, "I see people; they look like trees walking around."

Once more Jesus put his hands on the man's eyes. Then his eyes were opened, his sight was restored, and he saw everything clearly.

MARK 8:22-25

In the above portion of Scripture there are some things Jesus did that we should keep in mind as we heal the sick. Not even in the ministry of Jesus was there always an instantaneous healing. There are some essential things to remember when that is the case.

- **Jesus led the blind man outside the village.** It's always a good idea to get away from the unbelief and commotion. Normally, Jesus would just speak a simple word of authority and the person would be healed, but Jesus recognized that the man needed some special attention, so he took the man to a better environment outside the village.

- **Know what you're praying for.** Jesus knew that the man was blind, so he took him outside the village to pray for the man's eyes. Know what mountain has to be removed. In this case it is blindness. Don't assume you know the situation—ask.

- **Always ask the person "How do you feel?"** After Jesus prayed for the man, he asked him "Do you see anything?" You will want to know if the person is healed and if not, you will know to pray again—as Jesus did.

- **Know if the healing is full or partial.** The man answered Jesus, "I see people; they look like trees walking around." By his answer, Jesus knew that the man only had a partial healing.

- **If needed, do it again.** Jesus knew that the man was not entirely healed, so he prayed again, "Once more Jesus put his hands on the man's eyes. Then his eyes were opened, his sight was restored, and he saw everything clearly" (verse 25).

After you ask a person if they are healed, and if they are not, lay your hands on them and speak again. This is incredibly important; it could take several times before the person is totally healed.

Ask the person you prayed for to get up and walk around and check things out and tell everyone in the meeting exactly how they feel and whether or not they were healed. Don't be afraid to put yourself on the spot in asking such a question, for we don't do the healing anyway—God does. We're just the person praying for the healing. If you put yourself on the spot by asking the person, "How do you feel?" there will be an increase in healing because you will be demonstrating a higher level of faith. Don't worry about results, the results will come.

> DON'T WORRY ABOUT RESULTS, THE RESULTS WILL COME

In Acts 3:1-10, Peter and John prayed for a man who was crippled from birth, and they said to the man, "In the name of Jesus Christ of Nazareth, walk." But after declaring "walk," they took the man "by the right hand, helped him up, and instantly the man's feet and ankles became strong. He jumped to his feet and began to walk."

To take someone by the hand and help them up is an act of faith, and should be done without forcing the issue, but this is exactly what Peter and John did with the crippled beggar. He had been crippled from birth and had no idea what it felt like to walk, so Peter and John helped him get started.

Prayer In Healing

Prayer is important in healing the sick, however, there is no record in the New Testament of anyone praying over the sick for healing. It is always done in conjunction with a word (or words) of authority, the laying on of hands, in Jesus' name. Prayer is important in that it prepares us to heal the sick; this preparation is critical in the outcome of healing.

In some instances the disciples would pray directly beforehand or they would give an explanation beforehand, but it was never just prayer for healing the sick. Jesus gave us power and authority to *"Heal the sick, raise the dead, cleanse those who have leprosy, drive out demons"* (Matthew 10:8, Luke 9:1).

The following are some examples shown in Scripture of how prayer played an important part in healing, but it was always a word of authority and/or laying on of hands that actually did the healing:

The Apostle Paul was on the Island of Malta after being in a shipwreck. While at the home of the chief official of the island, he found out that the chief official's father was sick. Paul went in to see him, then prayed, placed his hands on him, and healed him (Acts 28:8).

Paul prayed beforehand, then laid hands on the chief official's father. Paul didn't pray for the healing. He prayed, then after prayer Paul laid hands on him and healed him with a word of authority.

When Jesus prayed to bring Lazarus back to life, he prayed aloud from outside the tomb for the benefit of the people:

> *Jesus looked up and said, "Father, I thank you that you have heard me. I knew that you always hear me, but I said this for the benefit of the people standing here, that they may believe that you sent me."*
>
> *After Jesus gave an explanation to the people, he called in a loud voice, "Lazarus, come out!" The dead man came out, his hands and feet wrapped with strips of linen, and a cloth around his face.*
>
> JOHN 11:41-44

The same is true of Peter and John healing the lame beggar at the gate called Beautiful.

> *Silver or gold I do not have, but what I do have I give you. In the name of Jesus Christ of Nazareth, walk.*
>
> ACTS 3:6

Peter had learned from Jesus how to heal the sick, so when he healed the lame beggar, he did exactly what he was taught. Peter gave an explanation to the lame man then healed him with a word of authority.

Also, when Peter was in the city of Joppa, he healed a woman named Tabitha:

> *He got down on his knees and prayed. Turning toward the dead woman, he said, "Tabitha, get up." She opened her eyes, and seeing Peter she sat up.*
>
> ACTS 9:40

Jesus, Paul, and Peter each prayed beforehand in these references, then used words of authority and/or the laying on of hands to raise the dead, and heal the sick and lame.

What confuses this issue of praying for the sick is what it says in James 5:14-15:

> *Is any one of you sick? He should call the elders of the church to pray over him and anoint him with oil in the name of the Lord. And the prayer offered in faith will make the sick person well; the Lord will raise him up.*

Certainly, it's important to pray. James was saying for the church to pray, and there are many things that one could pray for related to healing, but **it is always accomplished through a word of authority and/or laying on hands done in Jesus' name.**

Here is an example requiring prayer. A man brought his son to the disciples for healing and they could not heal him. They later wanted to know why they couldn't heal the boy, and Jesus replied:

> *This kind can come out only by prayer.*
>
> MARK 9:29

Jesus was declaring that with the tough cases there had to be prayer in order to have success.

When a word of authority isn't enough to heal someone, you then sit them down and pray. It may take some time, so it is important to be persistent and patient until there are results. Prayer used in conjunction with a word (or words) of authority and/or the laying on of hands is the answer.

When healing the sick, we are expected to pray for them, not just use a word of authority, especially by the unbeliever (also some Christians). They don't expect you to just use a word of authority and be done with it. That is why using the Lazarus prayer (explained in the following section) is useful when praying for someone unfamiliar with the Gospel.

Prayer is always important in what God is doing, and in the outcome of our life as disciples. Sometimes it is necessary to pray until things are shaken as when the disciples prayed in Acts 4:31:

> *After they prayed, the place where they were meeting was shaken. And they were all filled with the Holy Spirit and spoke the word of God boldly.*

THE LAZARUS PRAYER

When we see some people pray for the sick on TV or in a local church, or home group, each person has their own way of praying for the sick. We sometimes think that some people have an ulterior motive—hyper-spirituality, showmanship, or to attract a crowd. However, most of the time they are sincere. It's okay to use a little showmanship on occasion; even Jesus did that. However, most of the time Jesus would tell the person, "Don't tell anyone," but they would go and tell others anyway, and the news about Him would spread.

The healing of Lazarus is the longest account of any healing and the most dramatic of all the healing that Jesus did.

Jesus intentionally took his time getting to Lazarus' tomb.

> *When he heard that Lazarus was sick, he stayed where he was two more days.*

JOHN 11:6

The healing of Lazarus is an example of an intentional strategy, Jesus wanted to demonstrate that a person dead and buried could be brought back to life, so that after his own death, the people would have faith to believe in his resurrection, and also that the dead in Christ will rise. He explains to his disciples that Lazarus is dead, and says:

For your sake I am glad I was not there, so that you may believe.

JOHN 11:15

On the way to the tomb Jesus has a conversation with Martha:

"Your brother will rise again." Martha answered, "I know he will rise again in the resurrection at the last day."

Jesus said to her, "I am the resurrection and the life. He who believes in me will live, even though he dies; and whoever lives and believes in me will never die. Do you believe this?"

Jesus indicates His motives here by declaring that he is the resurrection, and the raising of Lazarus is a foreshadowing of his own resurrection.

When Jesus finally arrived at the tomb, Lazarus had been in the tomb for four days; when they took the stone away, Jesus prayed. But he didn't pray for the healing of Lazarus, he prayed:

Father, I thank you that you have heard me. I knew that you always hear me, but I said this for the benefit of the people standing here, that they may believe that you sent me.

JOHN 11:41-42

Jesus used this prayer to explain the Kingdom to the people assembled and listening to him. As an example: Say you notice a co-worker limping at the job and you ask if you can pray for him. If he is not a believer or church goer, and has no understanding of the Gospel, you would pray in such a way that would give him some understanding of the Gospel. You would pray in this manner: "Dear Lord, I thank you that you want to heal Fred because your love for him is immeasurable. I thank you that when you shed your blood for salvation that you had Fred in mind. Touch him Lord—body, soul, and spirit—heal his body and bring him into a personal relationship with you, so that he might lead life to the fullest. You really want to see him healed from this pain, but most of all Lord, you want him to be part of your Kingdom. So, Lord, I ask that you display your love for Fred by healing him. Also, heal his relationships, take away his worries, and give him the peace that you promise to all that are yours. I declare his body to be healed, in Jesus' name."

This is a sample of the way you would pray for someone who doesn't know the Lord. It is a way of taking the opportunity to explain the Gospel.

> PRAYING FOR HEALING IS AN OPPORTUNITY TO SHARE THE GOSPEL

Perhaps Fred had no idea that God loved him and wanted to heal him. Maybe Fred never knew that God wanted him in his Kingdom, and that God would heal his relationships, or that God desired a personal relationship with him, or that God would give him peace. But, as you were praying for Fred's healing you took the opportunity to convey the Gospel message to him.

A type of Lazarus prayer was prayed by Peter when he and John encountered the lame beggar at the Gate Beautiful. First, Peter said, "Look at us!" (Acts 3:5). Peter wanted to get the man's attention because he was about to do something that would change the lame beggar's life forever, and Peter wanted the man's full attention, and gave him some explanation of what was about to happen.

Then Peter said, "Silver or gold I do not have, but what I do have I give you."

ACTS 3:6

Peter wanted the man to know that what he was about to receive was not something from the world, nor could it be bought. It was not silver or gold, but something more valuable. It was a present from a loving God who wanted to bless him by restoring his legs. It was something that Peter had received freely and was about to give freely.

Peter's prayer at the Gate Beautiful is similar to the Lazarus prayer in that it gives an explanation before words were spoken to heal the man: "In the name of Jesus Christ of Nazareth, walk."

Unbelievers appreciate prayer even if they don't get healed because they have never had that done for them; besides, this will give you a chance to pray the Lazarus prayer over them. When the opportunity presents itself to pray for someone, by all means give freely.

Signs, wonders, and miracles, if used strategically can accomplish a great deal. In the healing of Lazarus, Jesus used the opportunity to:

- Gather a crowd.
- Present a Gospel message (through the Lazarus prayer).
- Impart faith to those present.
- Foretell of his own resurrection from the grave.

So when you see some ministers that are a little too flamboyant—tending to attract attention because of exuberance, confidence, and stylishness—for your taste, just remember that in the healing of Lazarus, Jesus was also a little flamboyant (if that's the proper term). It's okay to use signs, wonders, and miracles strategically. Jesus even put the healing of Lazarus on his own timetable to suit his strategy. He didn't rush to the tomb to free Lazarus.

DON'T ARGUE WITH GOD

When Moses and the Israelites were trapped between the Red Sea and Pharaoh's army who wanted to destroy Israel (Exodus 14:15), Moses cried out to the Lord. The Lord replied by saying, *"Why are you crying out to me? Tell the Israelites to move on."* The Lord wanted them to stop crying out to him, and do what he had already told them to do.

There is a time to pray, and there is a time to do what the Lord has already told you to do. The time had come for Moses to stop crying out (praying) and to start following the Lord's instructions:

> *Raise your staff and stretch out your hand over the sea to divide the water so that the Israelites can go through the sea on dry ground.*
>
> EXODUS 14:16

The Bible says that we are to "pray in the Spirit on all occasions with all kinds of prayers and requests" (Ephesians 6:18). However, there are times we don't have to pray, but swing into action.

If God says that it's not necessary to pray, then it is one of those occasions that we should not pray, and just take action. It would have been foolish for Moses to stand at the edge of the Red Sea and argue with God, saying, *"But God I want to pray."* If Moses had insisted on praying, the Red Sea may not have ever parted for him.

There is also an occasion in the New Testament where Jesus says to speak to an issue, and it is not necessary to pray:

> *I tell you the truth, if you have faith as small as a mustard seed,* ***you can say to this mountain****, 'Move from here to there' and it will move.*
>
> MATTHEW 17:20 *(Author Emphasis)*

When we encounter a mountain, we don't have to say, "Please God, remove this mountain." We can be assured that the mountain will respond to the word we speak, and be removed.

When mountains are removed, people are set free from all manner of things. A lady had panic attacks (a mountain) that would cripple her emotionally, and they would come on her every day, brought on by the most insignificant incidents. Attacks would be brought on by just leaving the house, shopping, driving, or being around strangers. God healed her and she was set free from that mountain of fear in her life.

A word of authority goes from top to bottom, from the summit to the root system.

I was ministering at a men's meeting in a foreign city, and it was a tremendously long healing service. At the end of the meeting a man brought up his little daughter on the stage. She had a paralyzed hand. It was a mountain in the life of that little girl and to her father. It was the last day of the men's meeting, and the men were saying their goodbyes to one another, many had come from long distances to attend. The father; of the little girl was speaking to me in Spanish. So, I called over my interpreter and he told me that the girl had a paralyzed hand and was going in for surgery the next day. We simply took authority over the mountain of paralysis, the mountain was immediately removed, and the child was healed.

We had many men healed that day, but I don't recall the details of any of them, except the little girl. It's amazing how the ones that we'll remember are the children, and these are the ones that will really touch our heart.

In Jesus' ministry, he healed people with a word of authority. There are no examples of him doing any pre-counseling, breaking of curses, binding and losing, dealing with issues or repentance (until after they had been healed). Why is it that there is no record in the New Testament of anyone (Jesus, Peter, Paul, Philip, etc.) sitting someone down, counseling them, and praying over them?

The understanding of moving a mountain or mulberry tree is significant. It points to the reason that it is unnecessary to use all the non-biblical teachings and methods used today in healing the sick and deliverance. The only thing necessary is to follow the model seen in the New Testament, the same method which Jesus, Peter, and Paul used.

THE FINGER OF GOD

Jesus tells us how demons are driven out:

If I drive out demons by the finger of God, then the Kingdom of God has come upon you.

LUKE 11:20

Jesus is the pattern for all that we do and if he drove out demons by the finger of God, then so do we. The finger of God is not just a power source that aids in dealing with demons. The finger of God is the Holy Spirit, as Jesus clarifies in Matthew 12:28:

> *It is by the Spirit of God that I drive out demons, then the Kingdom of God has come upon you.*

Although the finger of God is recognized as the Holy Spirit, it is also the Father and Son. It is the totality of God that drives out demons. The finger of God touches the spot that needs to be touched, and the power of God is released through that touch. Hence, the Kingdom of God has come upon that place.

It is the same finger of God that inscribed the Ten Commandments on the two stone tablets:

> *When the Lord finished speaking to Moses on Mount Sinai, he gave him the two tablets of the covenant law, the tablets of stone inscribed by the finger of God.*
>
> EXODUS 31:18

And it's the same fingers that wrote on the plaster wall during King Belshazzar's banquet (Daniel 5:5-6), which scared him so badly that he became weak and his knees knocked. They were specific prophetic words that the hand wrote, which spoke of King Belshazzar's demise and the end of his kingdom; it was carried out immediately by an invasion of the Medes and Persians.

The hand (finger) of God, because it is God's hand, doesn't do things indiscriminately, it knows exactly what to do, and how to do it. As we speak a word of authority, the most efficient, effective way is carried out by the Holy Spirit.

Authority has been granted to us, the Christian, and sealed forever. We just appropriate it by faith and as we do, the finger of God does the rest.

Jesus gave Christians incredible authority over evil. When Jesus was questioned about his authority, he answered by asking a question:

> *The chief priests and the teachers of the law, together with the elders, came up to him. "Tell us by what authority you are doing these things," they said. "Who gave you this authority?" He replied, "I will also ask you a question. Tell me, John's baptism—was it from Heaven, or from men?"*
>
> LUKE 20:2-4

This is the question we have to ask ourselves, and unquestionably come to the conclusion that it is from Heaven. Christians have the highest authority possible—from Heaven, and it has been given to us by Jesus. He and all of Heaven stands behind it:

> *For in Christ all the fullness of the Deity lives in bodily form, and **you have been given fullness in Christ,** who is the head over every power and authority."*
>
> COLOSSIANS 2:9-10

Authority was lost in the garden—through sin—but regained at the cross through Christ's death and resurrection. However, even now, it can be stolen from us through deceptions:

> *See to it that no one takes you captive through hollow and deceptive philosophy, which depends on human tradition and the basic principles of this world rather than on Christ.*
>
> COLOSSIANS 2:8

Jesus has given us authority over all the power of the enemy (Luke 10:19). Let me emphasize that it says we have authority over "**all**" the power of the enemy. It also says, "**Nothing** will harm you." Demons will bluff, bluster, and try to intimidate, but Christians are the ones with the authority and power as the finger of God does what needs to be done in healing and deliverance.

> BE ASSURED, WHATEVER MOUNTAIN YOU SPEAK TO WILL RESPOND TO THE WORD AND BE REMOVED

Chapter Ten

Persistence

Some people are not healed because they give up too soon. If you are willing to spend the time, healing will happen. When a word of authority doesn't bring the desired healing, then it is time to persist in prayer (and authority) for the individual.

Jesus taught his disciples on the importance of persistence when he said:

> *Suppose you have a friend, and you go to him at midnight and say, "Friend, lend me three loaves of bread; a friend of mine on a journey has come to me, and I have no food to offer him." And suppose the one inside answers, "Don't bother me. The door is already locked, and my children and I are in bed. I can't get up and give you anything." I tell you, even though he will not get up and give you the bread because of friendship, yet **because of your shameless audacity** he will surely get up and give you as much as you need.*
>
> Luke 11:5-8

The man in bed didn't get up because the man was his friend, it was because of the "shameless audacity" from the man who wanted the bread that caused the man to get up and give him the bread he wanted.

This Spripture is telling us to press through to the conclusion of the healing, even using "shameless audacity" in our attempt to get someone healed. Let me emphasize that when a word of authority doesn't work, turn to "Plan B," which is to continue to administer healing until it is manifested.

The Canaanite woman kept crying out after Jesus and because she did, Jesus healed her daughter. She ignored what Jesus said about being sent only to the lost sheep of Israel:

> *A Canaanite woman from that vicinity came to Him, crying out, "Lord, Son of David, have mercy on me! My daughter is demon-possessed and suffering terribly." Jesus did not answer a word. So his disciples came to him and urged him, "Send her away, for she keeps crying out after us." He answered, "I was sent only to the lost sheep of Israel."*
>
> MATTHEW 15:22-24

She didn't walk away or give up when Jesus did not respond in the affirmative. She persisted, "kept crying out," and received what she wanted—the healing for her daughter.

Blind Bartimaeus is another person who persisted until he got his healing:

> *When he heard that it was Jesus of Nazareth, he began to shout, "Jesus, Son of David, have mercy on me!" Many rebuked him and told him to be quiet, but he shouted all the more, "Son of David, have mercy on me!"*
>
> MARK 10:47-48

Jesus called Bartimaeus and healed him, but what if Bartimaeus didn't persist in shouting—would he have been healed? We don't know for sure, but probably not. The shouting demonstrated the level of Bartimaeus' faith, and God will respond to persistent faith.

A woman who owned the house where Elijah stayed had a son who suddenly became ill and died. She called for Elijah, who took the boy in his arms and carried him to an upper room, and placed the boy on the bed. He then:

Stretched himself out on the boy three times and cried out to the Lord, "Lord my God, let this boy's life return to him!"

1 KINGS 17:20

The boy's life returned to him, and Elijah carried the boy down to his mother —alive. What would have happened if Elijah had cried out to the Lord only two times, instead of three? Would the boy have lived? Probably not!

When someone is not healed it is difficult, if not impossible, to figure out why. I suggest you not think that you have to have every answer, but know that the ultimate answer is to persist in prayer, faith, power, and authority. If you try to figure things out and fail, you will be inclined to quit, but if your intention is to persist without over-thinking things, it is much more effective. Remember, keep it simple!

I recently got a phone call from a woman I knew from another state who was sobbing on the phone. She had been dealing with Lyme disease for a long time and had many friends, church members, and pastors praying for her without success. Her condition was severe and she didn't know what to do; she said that she had tried everything. I told her that there was one thing that she hadn't tried yet, and that was to persist in prayer, faith, power, and authority, until she was healed. When nothing seems to be working, it's time to get serious and to know that God will heal you if you persist in prayer and repentance.

We should believe that a word of authority will heal the sick, but if it is not enough, we should then be willing to persist in prayer. We should set daily or weekly appointments to pray for the person who needs healing.

Most of the time healing is relatively simple, as noted in Spripture. However, some healing will take persistence and effort, and everyone involved should be determined to persist until there are results.

A Progressive Healing

It is sometimes discouraging when we pray for someone and they aren't healed instantaneously, but we shouldn't be discouraged. After all, even in Jesus' ministry, there were times when there was not an instantaneous healing. A case in point is in Mark 8:22-25 when Jesus had to pray again to restore a blind man's sight:

> *Jesus asked the blind man, "Do you see anything?"*
>
> *He looked up and said, "I see people; they look like trees walking around."*
>
> *Once more Jesus put his hands on the man's eyes. Then his eyes were opened, his sight was restored, and he saw everything clearly.*

The way that Jesus phrased this question ("Do you see anything?") leads me to believe that Jesus expected the man's healing to be partial (or in progress). It's important to find out what the status of the healing is so you know what to do next. After the man responded, "I see people;

they look like trees walking around," Jesus once more put his hands on the man's eyes. It was then that he was totally healed.

Another progressive healing was when Jesus prayed for the ten men who had leprosy:

> *As he was going into a village, ten men who had leprosy met him. They stood at a distance and called out in a loud voice, "Jesus, Master, have pity on us!" When he saw them, he said, "Go, show yourselves to the priests." And as they went, they were cleansed.*
>
> LUKE 17:12-13

They were healed as "they went"—not instantaneously. Which means that after praying for someone, we are to continue to believe in faith and allow the Holy Spirit to finish his work.

We also see healing as a progression in the Old Testament when Elisha prayed for the widow's son:

> *Elisha said to Gehazi, "Tuck your cloak into your belt, take my staff in your hand and run. If you meet anyone, do not greet him, and if anyone greets you, do not answer. Lay my staff on the boy's face." Gehazi went on ahead and laid the staff on the boy's face, but there was no sound or response. So Gehazi went back to meet Elisha and told him, "The boy has not awakened."*
>
> *When Elisha reached the house, there was the boy lying dead on his couch. He went in, shut the door on the two of them and prayed to the LORD. Then he got on the bed and laid upon the boy, mouth to mouth, eyes to eyes, hands to hands. As he stretched himself out upon him, the boy's body grew warm. Elisha turned away and walked back*

and forth in the room and then got on the bed and stretched out upon him once more. The boy sneezed seven times and opened his eyes."

2 KINGS 4:29-35

1. Verse 29, Elisha told Gahazi to lay his staff on the boy's face (no instantaneous healing).

2. Verse 33, Elisha shut the door and prayed to the Lord (no instantaneous healing).

3. Verse 34, Elisha got on the bed and lay upon the boy, mouth to mouth, eyes to eyes, hands to hands. As he stretched himself out upon him, the boy's body grew warm (no instantaneous healing, however, the warmth in the boy's body would normally indicate the beginning of a healing).

4. Verse 35, Elisha turned away and walked back and forth in the room and then got on the bed and stretched out upon him once more. The boy sneezed seven times and opened his eyes.

Finally the boy was healed, but it wasn't without repeated prayer in various forms.

Faith believes, regardless of what you see happening or not happening. If you pray for someone and they are not instantaneously healed, your obligation is to continue to believe, and to encourage the person to continue to believe. I have often seen people healed, in church, after they return to their seat, or the next day or that next week, and sometimes it is only when they return to their doctor for an examination, is it made clear that they are healed.

Faith believes even when there is no evidence because faith is being *"Certain of what we do not see"* (Hebrews 11:1). There doesn't have to be any evidence of the healing for you to believe; continue to trust God.

I walked into a church on a Sunday morning where I was going to preach and minister in healing the sick, and a lady approached, and held out her hands for me to see. She began telling me how the last time I was in that church, I had prayed for her hands that were badly deformed from arthritis. She told me that when the meeting was over I asked for a showing of hands of those who were healed. Since almost everyone raised their hands, I asked for anyone who didn't get healed to raise their hand. She raised her hand because she wasn't healed.

She said that she felt that it was a lack of faith to raise her hand, but she was being honest. I told her that it was okay for her to raise her hand; for the reality was that she wasn't healed … yet. However, she went on to tell me that she was healed later in the week. Her hands were so deformed that they couldn't function, but now they were completely healed and without any deformity. She answered correctly when asked if she was healed, but she believed for her healing, and she was healed later that week. It was a progressive healing.

Healing can be a process that may take an hour, overnight, or a few days, as in the case of King Hezekiah who was healed after three days (2 Kings 20:4-6):

> *Before Isaiah had left the middle court, the word of the LORD came to him: "Go back and tell Hezekiah, the ruler of my people, 'This is what the LORD, the God of your father David, says: I have heard your prayer and seen your tears; I will heal you. On the third day from now you will go up to the temple of the LORD. I will add fifteen years to your life.'"*

When someone is prayed for, let the healing percolate, and let God finish. When the person has a sickness as is the case of MS, Crohn's disease, COPD, heart defects, etc., but if they are without pain, it is hard to determine if they are healed or not. It is when they go back to their doctor for an examination that they realize that they have been healed.

Always pray again for the person when they are not healed immediately, as in the case of Jesus praying for the blind man (Mark 8:22-25), or Jesus praying for the demoniac (Mark 5:2-13), or in the case of Elisha praying for the boy (2 Kings 4:28-35). Many times the person will get a full healing after the second to fourth time that they are prayed for using a word of authority.

Don't Depend on How You Feel

I once ministered at an evening church service, and after the service, the pastor was driving me back to the hotel where I was staying. He said to me, "I know when it's time for me to pray for the sick when I feel heat on my hands, and they get oily, so I can feel this hot oily sensation."

I thought to myself, "Gee, I don't feel anything, but I wish I did." But, then I said, "Pastor, I really have never felt anything like that, but I think that I could go into the lobby of that hotel, and have a healing service just like we had in your church." I wasn't being arrogant, but wanted to make the point that I just don't feel anything when I pray for the sick, and we don't have to feel anything.

Some people feel heat, or oil on their hands, or have some other manifestation when they are about to pray for the sick. This is a sign to them that it is time to pray for the sick, and that they will have success in doing so. I don't feel anything when I am about to pray for the sick, and I don't think I ever have. I see things, on occasion, like tremors, or a shaking, or what appears to a shadow passing through the room, or something coming off the person. But you should never depend on feeling something or seeing something as you pray for the sick. The only things to pay attention to is what the Spriptures say and what the Holy Spirit is doing.

Another time, I was having a healing service in Mexico. Many people were in the line with all kinds of ailments, and a young boy was sitting on the stage next to me watching as I was ministering. After the meeting I had dinner with the boy's parents and my interpreter (Pastor Dave Hardy). At dinner, the boy was telling us that during the healing service, as I was praying for people, he could hear bones cracking and grinding. I didn't hear anything, and neither did Dave. But God allowed the boy to hear the bones grind and crack, probably to build his faith.

> THERE IS NOTHING THAT QUALIFIES US FOR THE MINISTRY OF SIGNS, WONDERS, AND MIRACLES

There is nothing that qualifies us for the ministry of signs, wonders, and miracles, but if I had to point to one Spripture that I thought might qualify anyone, it would be 1 Corinthians 1:27, where it says:

> *Think of what you were when you were called. Not many of you were wise by human standards; not many were influential; not many were of noble birth.* **But God chose the foolish things of the world to shame the wise;** *God chose the weak things of the world to shame the strong. God chose the lowly things of this world and the despised things—and the things that are not—to nullify the things that are.*

The Lord chose a certain kind of people to carry out his will. If you feel like you fall into the group of "foolish things of the world," and "the weak things of the world," you're probably right, but you're in good company. When the Lord called Gideon, he called him a "mighty warrior." Gideon was no mighty warrior at that time, but the Lord was speaking to what he was going to make Gideon into. He will take the "foolish things of the world" and the "weak things of the world" and turn them into mighty warriors.

Christians are anointed by the Holy Spirit to heal the sick, and as long as you belong to that unique group called the "foolish things," you qualify. If you look at the super-heroes of the Bible, they all qualify to belong to the "foolish things" group also:

- King David was an adulterer and a murderer.
- Peter disowned Jesus three times.
- Paul was a persecutor of the saints.

They each became heroes of the Bible because they were changed by the power of the Holy Spirit.

IN HIS HOMETOWN

I often hear of Christians going to the mission field and performing all manner of healing and miracles, but when they get back to their home churches among their own people, there is very little evidence of the miraculous. There are reasons why this happens. Oftentimes healing occurs on the mission field because of the level of expectation and faith of the people being ministered to, but that same faith or expectancy isn't present in their home church.

Such was the case of Jesus who couldn't do any miracles in his hometown because there was a familiarity, and consequently, they viewed Jesus as the carpenter. Jesus is the most gifted healer ever. There is no one even close to His giftedness in healing, yet he had trouble healing the sick in his hometown. He could only heal a few sick people because of their lack of faith.

A pastor friend of mine just got back from Africa and was very excited about the healing and miracles that he saw there. But chances are he will not necessarily see the same level of healing and miracles in his own church. However, the expectancy and atmosphere for consistent healing and miracles can be cultivated in any church.

When ministering in a third world country, expect to see miracles when praying for the sick. Be advised, you also might see some wild manifestations of evil.

This next story may be offensive to some; it has to do with some gross manifestations of evil that I heard first-hand from the person in the story.

I was in Florida when I met Apostle Isaiah from Africa. He was in Florida visiting the church where I was ministering in over the weekend. Isaiah told the story about his home church in Africa where he was preaching to about 1200 people on a Sunday morning when a witch doctor came in the back door. The witch doctor walked along the back of the sanctuary, walked along the side of the church, and came right up front to where Isaiah was preaching. Isaiah was preaching his message and didn't pay attention to the witch doctor. The witch doctor pulled open his shirt, cut himself open, and pulled out his intestines; he then put them back and healed himself. With that, he walked back along the side wall, across the back of the sanctuary, and out the front door. Isaiah just kept preaching.

Some time later on another Sunday morning, Isaiah was preaching, and the witch doctor again walked in the back door. He walked along the back wall, down the side wall, and walked up front to where Isaiah was preaching. Isaiah just kept delivering his message, ignoring the witch doctor. Again, the witch doctor pulls open his shirt, cuts himself open, and pulls out his intestines. And as the witch doctor is about to put his intestines back and heal himself, Isaiah interrupts his message, leans over toward the witch doctor, and says, "In Jesus' name you will not be healed." The witch doctor died on the spot.

This is a true story and from what I'm told, these kind of confrontations are not that uncommon in some places around the world. But the truth of the matter is, if or when it does happen, we have authority over all the power of the enemy, even in our home church. Whatever happens in a foreign country, in terms of the miraculous, can happen in our home church.

It must have been a tremendous disappointment to Jesus not being able to minister to the people of his hometown. Even though they were amazed at his teachings, they were offended because there was a familiarity with him and His family. They knew him as the carpenter—perhaps he did some carpentry work for some of them, putting on a roof, or building a table or chairs. A similar kind of familiarity can exist in our home church.

Mark records three places where Jesus had difficulty performing miracles:

Jesus left there and went to his hometown, accompanied by his disciples. When the Sabbath came, he began to teach in the synagogue, and many who heard him were amazed.

"Where did this man get these things?" they asked. "What's this wisdom that has been given him that he even does miracles! Isn't this

the carpenter? Isn't this Mary's son and the brother of James, Joseph, Judas and Simon? Aren't his sisters here with us?" And they took offense at him.

Jesus said to them, "Only in his hometown, among his relatives and in his own house is a prophet without honor." He could not do any miracles there, except lay his hands on a few sick people and heal them. And he was amazed at their lack of faith.

MARK 6:1-6

How could there ever be any signs, wonders, or miracles when they were offended at him? The fact that they took offense at Jesus, coupled with their lack of faith, shows that there was no way that they would see miracles. It didn't fit their understanding: they knew him as the carpenter, they knew his family, and these things didn't compute. It didn't fit into their religious understanding. They thought aloud, "Where would he get such things?"

It was actually hard for Jesus to do miracles in (1) his hometown, (2) among his relatives, and (3) in his own house (Mark 6:4). He could only heal a few sick people. It's common to hear ministers complain that they aren't as effective in healing people in their own church or home, as with strangers. They shouldn't feel bad because Jesus had the same problem. Jesus couldn't do miracles in his own "House," as in the same way the leader of a church might experience difficulty healing and doing miracles in his own church, unless the level of faith can be raised.

People in his hometown knew Jesus as the carpenter, as in a church where people know the pastor as counselor, preacher, etc. It has to do with familiarity, so when Jesus showed up with miraculous powers, they didn't know what to think of it. They still saw Jesus as the carpenter, and they couldn't get that out of their minds. This is what familiarity does; it causes people not to see the new person that God is using.

Years ago my Dad was in the hospital, and I went to visit him there. When I was ready to leave I prayed for him, and dad's roommate asked me to pray for him also. I don't know his name, but Dad called him Cotton. Cotton had tubes in his arm and nose and looked in bad shape. I was in a hurry, so I prayed and left immediately.

When I got home about an hour later, Dad called and sounded very excited. He told me that after I left the hospital room, their doctor came in and examined them. The doctor couldn't believe it but both men were completely fine, and he released them both from the hospital.

Praying for family members does work, so don't let familiarity with friends, family, or acquaintances discourage you from praying for the sick because some of the greatest miracles will come when you least expect it.

I think it would create a strange and unhealthy situation if all the family, friends, and acquaintances depended on you for healing all the time. They would probably cancel their health insurance and just depend on you to come and heal them when they had need. The healing minister would have a strange following of relatives and friends that depended on him for their health. And can you imagine the major problem you would have if a family member, friend, or acquaintance didn't get healed?

I've ministered to family members, and I could sometimes discern the unbelief. I know what it must have felt like when Jesus ministered in his hometown. Not that I compare myself with Jesus, but I could relate to the disappointment he must have felt. But don't let that stop you: they will appreciate it anyway, and it might be a case like Dad and Cotton who were both healed and released from the hospital in the same hour.

Jesus didn't frantically go from person to person in his hometown trying to heal them. Rather, he could discern those who had the faith to be healed, and he healed them. Faith can be seen in people (Matt 9:2, Luke 5:20), and Jesus saw the faith in people who wanted to be healed.

FAITH
BELIEVES
WHEN
THERE IS NO
EVIDENCE

Chapter Eleven

The Will of God

When I was in graduate school, our professor asked this question, "What is at the center of the universe?" Everyone had the right answer in saying "the Throne of God." Then he asked, "What is the central theme of the Throne of God?" There were many answers to this, ranging from a throne of judgment to mercy, to power, etc. There were a lot of answers from the students, but the professor called our attention to this Scripture:

> *Then I saw a Lamb, looking as if it had been slain, standing in the center of the Throne, encircled by the four living creatures and the elders.*
>
> Revelation 5:6

Our God is the God of all things, but the picture in Revelation 5:6, reveals him as a lamb, the God of love; love is his primary motivation, for *"God is love"* (1 John 4:8).

God is motivated by what he is, and he is love. When he healed the sick, oftentimes we read that his motivation was compassion:

- *"He had **compassion** on them and healed their sick."*

  MATTHEW 14:14 *(Author Emphasis)*

- *"Filled with **compassion,** Jesus reached his hand and touched the man."*

  MARK 1:41 *(Author Emphasis)*

- *"Jesus had **compassion** on them and touched their eyes. Immediately they received their sight and followed him."*

  MATTHEW 20:34 *(Author Emphasis)*

- *"When Jesus landed and saw a large crowd, he had **compassion** on them, because they were like sheep without a shepherd. So he began teaching them many things."*

  MARK 6:34 *(Author Emphasis)*

- *"I have **compassion** for these people; they have already been with me three days and have nothing to eat. If I send them home hungry, they will collapse on the way, because some of them have come a long distance."*

  MARK 8:2-3 *(Author Emphasis)*

- *"Jesus **wept**."*

  JOHN 11:35 *(Author Emphasis)*

Jesus **wept tears** for Lazarus, even though he knew that Lazarus was going to be raised from the dead. Jesus always had great compassion for the people. He even had compassion for people as he was facing rejection and the cross.

If we don't have compassion for people, we could be resounding gongs and clanging symbols because our motivation must be to serve people, not for the advancement of our reputation or ministry. It's never about advancing us, but it is always about serving God through serving his people.

When you minister to people, you won't necessarily feel an anointing, or a warm oil on your hands, or a burning on your hands like some do. I wish I did, but I don't. What is most important to feel as we minister to people is compassion for them. We should try to be pragmatic about healing, but even as we are doing that, we may, sometimes, have to fight back our emotions.

We must try to minister out of agape love (a commitment to others), and especially to those who need healing. Paul says this:

> *The only thing that counts is faith expressing itself through love.*
> GALATIANS 5:6

He is willing to heal because he is love, and he never refused anyone that came to him. It is his body, and he wants it healed! He wants a fully functioning body, without spot or wrinkle. When we heal, we are doing so for the purpose of healing his body. When one part suffers, we all suffer. We are serving his purpose when we heal whomever, whenever, however. That is what Jesus did for everyone who came to him.

IT IS THE WILL OF GOD

As we go to the Scriptures, it is easy to determine that signs, wonders, and miracles are the will of God. So, I will not spend a great deal of effort to show that; we should all know that God still heals people. Faith for healing; is dependent on knowing that it is the will of God to heal people. God does the healing, we are the ones that he uses for that ministry—all of us—not just some of us.

When Jesus heard that his disciples, including his apostles, could not heal a boy (John 17:17), he was very direct in his rebuke:

> *You unbelieving and perverse generation, ... how long shall I stay with you? How long shall I put up with you?*
>
> MATTHEW 17:17

When I read this passage, I feel as though Jesus was slightly perturbed. He definitely wanted his disciples to be able to heal that boy. They were the cream of the crop—the very disciples and apostles who followed him.

Faith comes by hearing the Word of God, so let me offer a few Scriptures that should allow us to have faith to heal the sick and be healed. Let's look in the Old Testament, where long before Jesus in bodily form appeared on the earth, Isaiah spoke of what Jesus would do for us:

> *He was despised and rejected by men, a man of sorrows, and familiar with suffering. Like one from whom men hide their faces he was despised, and we esteemed him not.*
>
> *Surely he took up our infirmities and carried our sorrows, yet we considered him stricken by God, smitten by him, and afflicted. "But he was pierced for our transgressions, he was crushed for our iniquities; the punishment that brought us peace was upon him, and by his wounds we are healed."*
>
> ISAIAH 53:3-5

Isaiah makes it abundantly clear that "he took up our infirmities," and "by his stripes we are healed. Healing was, and is the will of God.

> *He himself bore our sins in his body on the tree, so that we might die to sins and live for righteousness; by his wounds you have been healed.*

1 PETER 2:24

It is in the past tense, and has already been accomplished. What we need to do is appropriate it by faith. There is no "maybe" or "perhaps" or "if"—it has already been done.

The Old Testament and the New Testament agree that God heals our sicknesses and diseases; it is definitive that we are healed, as part of what Jesus accomplished. That could not be put any more succinctly than Peter puts it.

I feel it is unnecessary to offer these Scriptures as proof that God heals today because we should all know that he does. But in case there are some who are not sure, let me offer another one (the Bible is full of them):

> *Praise the LORD, O my soul; all my inmost being, praise his holy name. Praise the LORD, O my soul, and forget not all his benefits— who forgives all your sins and heals all your diseases, who redeems your life from the pit.*
>
> PSALMS 103:1-4

IF WE CAN BELIEVE FOR SALVATION, WE CAN BELIEVE FOR HEALING

If we can believe that we are free from sin by the sacrifice of Jesus on the cross, we can also believe for healing. They cannot be separated because he forgives our sins and heals our diseases, according to Isaiah 53 and Psalm 103. If we are not supposed to heal the sick, we then should not try to get anyone saved! That logic is simple—salvation and healing are linked together in redemption.

God is willing and able to heal our sickness and disease, but to believe that he is willing and able to heal is not enough. We must believe that God will heal us and heal others using us.

If God's will is to heal only some people, then none of us have any basis for faith unless we have a special revelation that we are among the favored ones.

If it were not the will of God to heal, why did he say, *"Greater things shall you do"*? If it were not his will for us to heal the sick, he would have said, "Greater things shall you do … except for healing the sick."

God doesn't get any glory from his people being sick, but he does get glory when people are healed by his power. God wants you healed and he wants you to heal others. The revealed will of God is for people to be healed and for you to be a healer (Mark 16:17-18). He desires all to be healed just as he desires for all to be saved.

A man with leprosy had a question for Jesus:

> *"Lord, if you are willing, you can make me clean." Jesus reached out his hand and touched the man.* **"I am willing,"** *he said. "Be clean!" Immediately he was cured of his leprosy."*
>
> MATTHEW 8:2-3 *(Author Emphasis)*

Those words from Jesus, *"I am willing,"* sum up the way Jesus feels about healing the sick. He is always willing, and he will not change his mind.

Jesus refers to healing and deliverance as the children's bread (Matthew 15:21-26). Bread is a basic nourishment, as is healing. Jesus, the bread of life in all that he provides for his children.

Those who don't believe that healing is for today are folks who say that the healing gift has passed away with the early church. They will sometimes pray for the sick, but have a difficult time believing or seeing people healed. People who believe that healing has passed away can be challenged by asking them to point to a Scripture that tells of its passing; they can't do it.

In this life no one escapes pain; suffering is part of life on earth. The world is full of people who are suffering from physical, psychological, and emotional pain—people who can be touched by a healing touch from God, through us.

Just as there is a great need for salvation, there is also a great need for healing—from older people with crippling arthritis and heart trouble, to crack babies born out of wedlock. Every person who needs healing can have it. Just as there is forgiveness from sin, there is also healing.

AN ACT OF GOD

There are occasions when someone has been healed, and there is no logical or theological explanation for it. It is just the sovereign will of God because he loves and is full of mercy and compassion, and it has nothing to do with our faith, authority, or prayer. It's simply that God wants to heal us, and there is no other explanation for it. It is an act of God!

People are sometimes healed during worship services, Sunday morning sermons, or just going about one's daily life. This is very exciting because it points out God's willingness to heal.

I was ministering in Toluca, Mexico, and after the last service when we were having dinner, Pastor Javier Rios got a phone call saying that one of his loyal parishioners was taken to the emergency room in serious condition. He asked me if I would go to the hospital with him to pray for the lady.

The room was very crowded where the woman was, so I went and started to pray for her. She looked to be in very serious condition; she had tubes in her and she was in a coma. I was praying for a few minutes when Javier came and joined me. We stood there praying, and after a few more minutes Javier said to me, "Brother Paul, this is the wrong woman." Javier then directed me to the correct woman on the other side of the crowded room, and we went over and prayed for her.

A few days after returning home to Texas, Javier called me and excitedly said, "Brother Paul, I had to call and tell you that both of those women that we prayed for in the hospital, were healed." In my opinion it was a sovereign move of God to heal the first woman. We didn't know her, we didn't even know if she was healed or even if she knew someone had prayed for her.

When my son, Clark, was a freshman in high school I was coaching him in the shotput (a 12 pound iron ball), and I was carelessly flipping the shot from hand to hand when it rolled off my left thumb in an awkward way causing a lot of pain. I thought it would better in a few days, but after a few weeks it was worse. I had it x-rayed but the doctor said he couldn't find anything. Then I had it looked at and x-rayed by another doctor, and nothing was found. Finally, I had another doctor look at it and x-rayed again, and he told me that the reason nothing was found in my hand or wrist was that the ligament in my thumb had torn off and was rolled up in my wrist.

I was in a lot of pain and had to sleep in a hand brace, because if I didn't and I moved the wrong way at night, the pain would wake me up. I was scheduled for surgery to reattach the ligament, when suddenly one morning, I realized that the pain was gone. I was completely healed. God sovereignly healed it.

From being an athlete for many years, I learned to live with pain and injuries without giving them a lot of thought beyond, "when can I get back in the game?" It wasn't my faith, or prayer, or authority that healed me, but the sovereign will of God.

God is sovereign and will display his power as he sees fit even if it doesn't fit our schedule, theology, or expectancy. Oftentimes during the praise and worship in a church service, people will be healed because healing is all about the presence of God, and him displaying his power.

As I began to speak, the Holy Spirit came on them as he had come on us at the beginning.

ACTS 11:15

… and the people all tried to touch him, because power was coming from him and healing them all.

LUKE 6:19

One day Jesus was teaching, and Pharisees and teachers of the law were sitting there. They had come from every village of Galilee and from Judea and Jerusalem. And the power of the Lord was with Jesus to heal the sick.

LUKE 5:17

About midnight Paul and Silas were praying and singing hymns to God, and the other prisoners were listening to them. Suddenly there was such a violent earthquake that the foundations of the prison were shaken. At once all the prison doors flew open, and everyone's chains came loose.

ACTS 16:25-26

There are times when you may not feel full faith for healing the sick, or that your faith is not up to par, or that your authority is in the dumper and you don't feel like praying, and God shows up in spite of the way you feel and he heals the sick person. Don't depend on how you feel, and don't neglect your duty to pray for the sick. It will amaze you what God will do through you even when you don't feel up to par.

WHO GETS THE CREDIT?

There is no extra credit for signs, wonders, and miracles when we get to Heaven. It isn't even a sign of maturity, although those that do them certainly could be mature believers. But the scariest thing of all is that someone could be doing signs, wonders, and miracles, and may not even be saved:

> *Not everyone who says to me, "Lord, Lord," will enter the Kingdom of Heaven, but only the one who does the will of my Father who is in Heaven. Many will say to me on that day, "Lord, Lord, did we not prophesy in your name and in your name drive out demons and in your name perform many miracles?" Then I will tell them plainly, "I never knew you. Away from me, you evildoers!"*
>
> MATTHEW 7:21-23

Those who say, *"Lord, Lord"* are saying the right thing, but they are not doing the right thing. But it is *"Everyone who hears these words of mine and puts them into practice is like a wise man who built his house on the rock"* (Matthew 7:24).

Doing the will of God is the main issue, and not the fact that we can perform miracles:

> *What, after all, is Apollos? And what is Paul? Only servants, through whom you came to believe—as the Lord has assigned to each his task. I planted the seed, Apollos watered it, but God has been making it grow. So neither the one who plants nor the one who waters is anything, but only God, who makes things grow. The one who plants and the one who waters have one purpose, and they will each be rewarded according to their own labor. For we are co-workers in God's service; you are God's field, God's building.*
>
> 1 CORINTHIANS 3:5-9

God raised up Pharaoh, the head of a nation, so that God could get glory from defeating him:

> *I raised you up for this very purpose, that I might display my power in you and that my name might be proclaimed in all the earth.*
>
> ROMANS 9:17

God will have mercy on whom he wants to have mercy, and he hardens whom he wants to harden.

When David slew Goliath, he did it with a small stone, not a brick or boulder, but a small stone with all the weight of God behind it.

In the Kingdom, there are no special places of honor, except the place Jesus occupies. We must be especially mindful of this when we are doing signs, wonders, and miracles because of the attention that might come our way, which could be destructive to us if we forget to give God the glory.

Ministry is not a place of honor, but it is a place of servanthood. Jesus was very critical of the teachers of the law and the Pharisees, and said this about them wanting to be honored:

Everything they do is done for people to see: They make their phylacteries wide and the tassels on their garments long; they love the place of honor at banquets and the most important seats in the synagogues; they love to be greeted with respect in the marketplaces and to be called "Rabbi'" by others.

MATTHEW 23:5-7

The teachers of the law and Pharisees were hypocritical phonies who were full of self importance.

Many times in the Scripture the Father says, *"You shall know that I am the Lord"* (1 Kings 20:28), because he wants everyone to know that he is God, and the best way to demonstrate that is by demonstrating his power. Because there is no other god that has any real power; there is no other religion that has any real power; and there are no other disciples of other gods that have any real power.

> NO OTHER GOD HAS ANY REAL POWER

Chapter Twelve

LET'S HAVE REVIVAL

When I attended the Toronto revival in Canada, I loved every minute of it. It had some strange manifestations with some people barking, roaring, clucking like a chicken, etc., but historically that's what happens during a genuine revival (demons get stirred up). However, the presence of God was so strong that there could be no denying that God was doing something special.

The worship was very powerful and the messages were simple. But after every service, the church workers would line people up and lay hands on them, and everyone would fall under the power of the Spirit, and lay on the floor until they were able get up.

Something happens when people go out under the power of the Spirit when someone lays hands on them; God only knows, but they get up feeling peaceful and refreshed. That is a good thing, and I love to go out in the Spirit. The times that I have fallen out by the power of the Spirit were awesome.

The people who were praying for others, generally speaking, did not expect a physical healing (at least I didn't see evidence of it), but were satisfied with seeing people fall out, and letting God take over. Even though there were no obvious healings that I saw, there was a demonstration of the power of God, as evidenced by people falling out in the Spirit. However, it would have been much more effective if it were obvious that people were getting healed.

It seemed that at almost every meeting, there were the doubters. They were the ones that would stand or sit in the back of the auditorium with their arms folded, taking it all in, but never joining in. The Pharisees, Sadducees, and the teachers of the law wouldn't accept the ministry of Jesus either. As in Jesus' day, the religious leaders of today (some, not all) will be the last to accept the end-time ministry of signs, wonders, and miracles.

America has had some awesome revivals; however, the end-time revival or (last day) harvest will be the greatest of all. It will have at least two distinct components: (1) it will include the greatest signs, wonders, and miracles the world has ever seen; and (2) it will not be a big star ministry carried out by the elite, but it will be a ministry of the Body of Christ carried out by everyone including the novice (Luke 10:17, Mark 16:17).

No church in America has yet reached the whole town or city (that I know of) in which it is located, yet there are examples in the Bible of just one miraculous healing, bringing revival to a whole town.

The crippled beggar at the Gate Beautiful, although it was only one healing is a good example of the harvest that is possible with just one significant healing. The town people *"recognized him as the same man who used to sit begging at the temple gate called Beautiful, and they were filled with wonder and amazement at what had happened to him"* (Acts

3:10). Many of the people knew that he was over forty years old and lame from birth.

So, Peter taking advantage of the opportunity, got up and preached a message about Jesus, and *"Many who heard believed; so the number of men who believed grew to about five thousand"* (Acts 4:4).

This healing at the Gate Beautiful was not the garden-variety, ordinary healing, but a very dramatic demonstration of the power of God. It brought a synergy to Peter's preaching, and because of that healing the people were eager to listen. The lame beggar became a walking, jumping, talking, billboard, advertising the Gospel of Jesus Christ.

I recently spoke with a pastor, who had two people healed at his church—one who was lame all of his life. They both got out of their wheelchairs and began walking, and his church exploded with growth.

However, we don't always have to see dramatic healings in order to see a great harvest. If the church just has simple healings on a consistent, verifiable, repeatable basis, it will get peoples' attention.

Signs, wonders, and miracles, will build the church by giving synergy to the preaching of the Word, and drawing an audience that is eager to listen.

LAST DAYS REVIVAL

We must first understand that Peter and others said those days were the last days; that is what he declared when he stood up on the day of Pentecost to address the crowd. He not only said it was the end-time, but he also said that the Holy Spirit would be poured out on all people:

"In the last days," *God says, "I will pour out my Spirit on all people."*
ACTS 2:17 *(Author Emphasis)*

The author of Hebrews also states that it is the last days:

> *In the past God spoke to our ancestors through the prophets at many times and in various ways, but* **in these last days** *he has spoken to us by his Son, whom he appointed heir of all things, and through whom also he made the universe.*
>
> HEBREWS 1:1-2 *(Author Emphasis)*

This Kingdom period we are currently in will see revival the likes of which have never been seen. Jesus said:

> *Go and* **make disciples of all nations,** *baptizing them in the name of the Father and of the Son and of the Holy Spirit, and teaching them to obey everything I have commanded you.*
>
> MATTHEW 28:19-20

The aim of revival is to have the people follow Jesus, not the preacher, evangelist, prophet, or apostle.

After the stoning of Stephen (Acts 7:59-60), the disciples scattered. Philip went down to a city in Samaria:

> *When the crowds heard Philip and saw the signs he performed, they all paid close attention to what he said. For with shrieks, impure spirits came out of many, and many who were paralyzed or lame were healed. So there was* **great joy in that city.**
>
> ACTS 8:6-8 *(Author Emphasis)*

Samaria had an awakening (revival) because they heard the Word preached and saw the demons dealt with and people healed.

When the Apostle Paul was shipwrecked on the island of Malta, the island's inhabitants—a whole people group—were convinced of the Gospel's validity by the healing of their sick (Acts 28:1-10).

Signs, wonders, and miracles, will convince skeptics of the Gospel's truth, but it will also bring a sense of revival among believers as in Luke 19:35-37, when Jesus was entering Jerusalem on a colt. It says:

> *As he went along, people spread their cloaks on the road. When he came near the place where the road goes down the Mount of Olives, the whole crowd of disciples began joyfully to* **praise God in loud voices for all the miracles they had seen.**
>
> LUKE 19:36-37 (Author Emphasis)

One miracle impacted a whole region as Peter visited Lydda and healed a paralytic named Aeneas:

> *As Peter traveled about the country, he went to visit the saints in Lydda. There he found a man named Aeneas, a paralytic who had been bedridden for eight years. "Aeneas," Peter said to him, "Jesus Christ heals you. Get up and take care of your mat." Immediately Aeneas got up.* **All those who lived in Lydda and Sharon saw him and turned to the Lord.**
>
> ACTS 9:32-35 (Author Emphasis)

All the people who lived in the two towns of Lydda and Sharon were impacted by that one miracle of healing. What Peter did in Lydda and Sharon is not the exception, but it is exactly what should happen through the average Christian.

The people of Joppa heard about what happened in Lydda, and asked Peter to come to Joppa to pray for a woman there who had died:

> *In Joppa there was a disciple named Tabitha (in Greek her name is Dorcas); she was always doing good and helping the poor. About that time she became sick and died, and her body was washed and placed in an upstairs room. Lydda was near Joppa; so when the disciples heard that Peter was in Lydda, they sent two men to him and urged him, "Please come at once!"*
>
> *Peter went with them, and when he arrived he was taken upstairs to the room. All the widows stood around him, crying and showing him the robes and other clothing that Dorcas had made while she was still with them.*
>
> *Peter sent them all out of the room; then he got down on his knees and prayed. Turning toward the dead woman, he said, "Tabitha, get up." She opened her eyes, and seeing Peter she sat up. He took her by the hand and helped her to her feet. Then he called for the believers, especially the widows, and presented her to them alive.* ***This became known all over Joppa, and many people believed in the Lord.***
>
> ACTS 9:36-42 (Author Emphasis)

When people see these kind of miracles they will respond and believe because it is hard to deny that God did it. So, Peter with two dramatic healings—one of Aeneas, a paralytic who had been bedridden for eight years, and Dorcas who had died, created great excitement in three cities.

Even among believers it will create excitement because experiencing miracles is not something that we get used to, it will always remain a source of excitement. The disciples praised God *"for all the miracles they had seen."* Seeing miracles will increase the faith of the disciples, bring excitement to the church, and build momentum for more miracles by creating an atmosphere of faith and expectancy. An environment charged with miracles and the presence of God is the atmosphere of revival. Prophesy can stir things inside the church as it says in 1 Corinthians 14:23-24:

If the whole church comes together and everyone speaks in tongues, and inquirers or unbelievers come in, will they not say that you are out of your mind? But if an unbeliever or an inquirer comes in while everyone is prophesying, they are convicted of sin and are brought under judgment by all, as the secrets of their hearts are laid bare. So they will fall down and worship God, exclaiming, "God is really among you!"

Prophesy is a powerful sign to the unbeliever "When the whole church comes together," and it will cause an unbeliever to "fall down and worship God." However, it is a sign primarily for inside the church walls as the "church comes together." It certainly can be used outside the church walls, but it is primarily a sign to be used "when the whole church comes together."

> PROPHECY IS A POWERFUL SIGN TO THE UNBELIEVER

We need a proactive church universal to emerge to bring large-scale revival, in order to correct all the ills in our society. There is no other answer. The government is getting more and more inept because of the political infighting and polarization (greed and lust) of the political parties.

God isn't a Democrat or a Republican and he doesn't need either party to do what he desires to do, but it depends on the miracle church to emerge.

Bible clubs won't do the job in subduing the earth, or bringing revival, but the church full of power will. A church full of power is when all the believers are ministering together in signs, wonders, and miracles in their sphere of authority.

THE KINGDOM

If we gauge the church's success in terms of the Great Commission, which is to make disciples of all nations, we will have to conclude that up to this time in history, the church has failed. Jesus said:

> *All authority in Heaven and on earth has been given to me. Therefore go and* ***make disciples of all nations.***
>
> MATTHEW 28:18 *(Author Emphasis)*

Is this wishful thinking on the part of Jesus to make disciples of all nations? No! It is a prophetic declaration of what will take place on earth. We are commissioned to make disciples of all nations, but when we compare the success of churches to what Jesus stated in the Great Commission, it is obvious we have a long way to go. We haven't even made disciples of many neighborhoods, let alone discipling of nations.

In the first command that the Father gave to Adam and Eve in Genesis 1:28, he said:

> *Be fruitful and increase in number; fill the earth and subdue it. Rule over the fish of the sea and the birds of the air and over every living creature that moves on the ground.*

He said to subdue the earth, which is basically the same thing Jesus said when he told us to *"make disciples of all nations."* Subduing the earth and making disciples of all nations is God's purpose for the church; all Christians have a part in this ministry.

Speaking to the Romans, the Apostle Paul declared that we are going to crush Satan, which is another way of saying that we, the church, are going to be dominant on the earth:

> *The God of peace will soon **crush Satan** under your feet.*
> ROMANS 16:20 *(Author Emphasis)*

The church should strengthen its people so they can strengthen the church, so that ultimately the Kingdom of God will increase. The Kingdom is built one Christian at a time. We all contribute to the building of the Kingdom. A good example of this is Peter's mother-in-law. Three times, Scripture gives the story of her being bedridden with a high fever (Matthew 8:14, Mark 1:30, Luke 4:38). Jesus healed her, and she got up and waited on Jesus. Part of her ministry was to serve, but if she were bedridden, she couldn't carry out her ministry. The same is true of any believer who is incapacitated; they cannot carry out their assignment and calling. That is a powerful reason for people to be healed.

It doesn't matter what our calling is, as long as we carry it out. Paul says we should try to excel in the gifts that build up the church (1 Corinthians 14:12). Paul says that prophecy will build up the church (1 Corinthians 14:4), however, signs, wonder, and miracles, also build up the church. It frees the saints who are bedridden, in pain, in hospitals, etc. to carry out the work of the ministry and it will convince the unbeliever that Jesus is the one and only true God. It authenticates the Gospel.

The church's purpose is all about building the Kingdom of God. It was a priority of Jesus, and it should be our priority. The purposes of spiritual gifts are for the building of the Kingdom of God, and we should not be ignorant of spiritual gifts. (1 Corinthians 12:1). God wants us to use spiritual gifts in the church and out in the marketplace to build the Kingdom.

Revival(s) will spontaneously happen when the masses see miracles. A missionary to Africa overheard a Muslim cleric saying that Africa was lost to Christianity because the Christians were doing miracles and they (the Muslims) couldn't do miracles.

Falling out under the power of the Spirit is a wonderful experience, but we must believe for more than this. We have to do more and believe for more.

There is a practical issue when healing the sick. In Mark 8 when Jesus healed the blind man, he asked him a question and determined that he needed to lay hands on him again to complete the healing. If the man had fallen out under the power of the Spirit, he would not have been able to answer Jesus' question. There is no record in Scripture of anyone falling out under the power of the Spirit while Jesus was praying for their healing.

Years ago, I was satisfied with seeing people fall out under the power of the Spirit. I liked doing that; it really is fun to see people fall out when you touch them. However, I was ministering at a service and when I prayed for the people with the laying on of hands, no one fell out under the power of the Spirit. I thought that something was drastically wrong, but when I inquired of God, he told me not to pray for people like that any more. He told me to sit the people down and hold their feet and pray for them that way. Perhaps that is not for everyone to pray like that, but that is the way I pray for people most of the time. Remember that healing is not a matter of technique, but a matter of faith.

As the church is restored to a place of power and glory, we will see novice revivals as the equipped saints do what they are called to do—

that is, to enter into signs, wonders, and miracles as part of their every day activity.

The revival of the future will be a function of the Body. It will be a signs, wonders, and miracles movement carried out by all Christians, using all manner of techniques to heal the sick. It will be a movement conducted by everyday, ordinary Christians who believe the Word.

In Matthew 17, a man brought his son to Jesus. He said that he brought his son to Jesus' disciples but they could not heal him. The disciples and apostles that followed Jesus could not heal the boy; Jesus' response was harsh. He said:

> *You unbelieving and perverse generation, ... how long shall I stay with you? How long shall I put up with you?*
>
> MATTHEW 17:17

Jesus addressed the whole group that was following him including disciples, apostles, young, old, men, women, and a whole generation who he called a perverse generation. He expected all who followed him to be able to heal the sick.

Revivals of the future will happen in large part because ordinary Christians full of faith will step forward; signs, wonders, and miracles will follow them, to the glory of God.

TESTING THE CARPENTER

Jesus had an interesting problem when he began his ministry. For most of his life he labored as a carpenter and he had no credentials, degrees, or fame. All of a sudden at age 30, with the help of John the Baptist, he was introduced to the masses. How was he going to do this? How could he attract large crowds? How could he impact a generation that would impact the world?

Many young ministers are called into the ministry with the thought of great success, but they soon find out that it's not as easy as expected. They think that if they just get into a pulpit, they will attract large crowds with their eloquence. Instead many struggle for years trying to support their family while ministering out of a rented storefront.

Jesus had instant success when he started his earthly ministry. In Matthew 3, John the Baptist baptized Jesus. In Matthew 4, Jesus was tempted by the devil. By the time we get to Matthew 4:23, Jesus is already beginning to impact the multitudes:

> *Jesus went throughout Galilee, teaching in their synagogues, proclaiming the good news of the Kingdom, and healing every disease and sickness among the people. News about him spread all over Syria, and people brought to him all who were ill with various diseases, those suffering severe pain, the demon-possessed, those having seizures, and the paralyzed; and he healed them. Large crowds from Galilee, the Decapolis, Jerusalem, Judea and the region across the Jordan followed him.*
>
> MATTHEW 4:23-25

It says, "News about him spread all over Syria, and large crowds followed…him." The carpenter, the Son of God, began his ministry, with preaching and teaching, and signs, wonders, and miracles.

This is the sequence that we see in Matthew 3-4 as Jesus entered his ministry:

1. The baptism in water and in the Holy Spirit (Matthew 3:14-17),

2. testing in the wilderness (Matthew 4:1-11),

3. the beginning of team building (Matthew 4:18-22),

4. and the model of ministry that followed (Matthew 4:23-25).

When John the Baptist tried to deter Jesus from being baptized by him, Jesus said, "Let it be so now; it is proper for us to do this to fulfill all righteousness." Being baptized by John was to fulfill "all righteousness," however, so was going into the desert to be tested.

He fulfilled "all righteousness" by being tested and demonstrating that neither the world nor Satan had any hold on him. Jesus had overcome the world, as he stated in John 16:33, *"I have overcome the world."* Jesus had to demonstrate how perfect he was for his ultimate ministry as the Lamb of God.

The three areas of testing of Jesus in the wilderness correspond to 1 John 2:16 where it says:

> *For everything in the world—the lust of the flesh, the lust of the eyes, and the pride of life—comes not from the Father but from the world.*

Satan tested Jesus in those three areas beginning with the lust of the flesh:

> *After fasting forty days and forty nights, he was hungry. The tempter came to Him and said, "If you are the Son of God, tell these stones to become bread."*
>
> *Jesus answered, "It is written: Man shall not live on bread alone, but on every word that comes from the mouth of God."*
>
> MATTHEW 4:2-4

Jesus was hungry after fasting forty days, but did not give in to the temptation of Satan by turning stones into bread, and thus he passed the lust of the flesh test.

Satan next tested Jesus in the pride of life:

Then the devil took him to the holy city and had him stand on the highest point of the temple. "If you are the Son of God," he said, "throw yourself down. For it is written: he will command his angels concerning you, and they will lift you up in their hands, so that you will not strike your foot against a stone."

Jesus answered him, "It is also written: 'Do not put the Lord your God to the test.'"

MATTHEW 4:5-7

Jesus could have thrown himself down and easily escaped without bodily harm, showing himself to all those in the city that he was special, but he wouldn't. Instead of listening to Satan, he refused, and thus he passed the pride of life test.

Finally, Satan tested Jesus in the lust of the eyes:

The devil took him to a very high mountain and showed him all the kingdoms of the world and their splendor:

"All this I will give you," he said, "if you will bow down and worship me." Jesus said to him, "Away from me, Satan! For it is written: 'Worship the Lord your God, and serve him only.'"

MATTHEW 4:8-10

And Jesus viewing all the kingdoms of the world rejected Satan's offer, and thus passed the "lust of the eyes" test.

Isaiah declared in the Old Testament that the Father would test Jesus:

*This is what the Sovereign Lord says: "See, **I lay a stone in Zion, a tested stone**, a precious cornerstone for a sure foundation; the one who relies on it will never be stricken with panic."*

ISAIAH 28:16 *(Author Emphasis)*

It was the plan of God from eternity to test Jesus, and to provide for us a pattern for all Christians to follow.

Satan had no hold on Jesus. He, therefore, walked in the fullness as the Messiah, and the fullness of signs, wonders, and miracles that he saw the Father doing. He tells us:

The prince of this world is coming. He has no hold over me, but he comes so that the world may learn that I love the Father and do exactly what my Father has commanded me.

JOHN 14:30-31

The flesh can't trust God for anything; flesh will trust the world for its provision.

We are all tested as Jesus was. This test will determine how much hold the world has on us. If the world has a strong hold on us, it will be more difficult to enter into doing signs, wonders, and miracles, because we will look to the world for validation, or we will trust the world for solutions. Consequently, we will not have the necessary faith to fully trust God.

This is what happened to Peter when he was walking on water, he failed when he saw the wind and the waves (a representation of the world).

As Jesus was walking toward the boat where His disciples were, he spoke to them saying:

> *Take heart; it is I. Do not be afraid. And Peter answered him, "Lord, if it is you, command me to come to you on the water." He said, "Come." So Peter got out of the boat and walked on the water and came to Jesus. But when he saw the wind, he was afraid, and beginning to sink he cried out, "Lord, save me."*
>
> MATTHEW 14:27-30

It was when he took his eyes off Jesus that he began to sink.

Christians are tested to see if they are free from the world's temptations, and be an instrument to be used for "special purposes":

> *In a large house there are articles not only of gold and silver, but also of wood and clay; some are for special purposes and some for common use. Those who cleanse themselves from the latter will be instruments for special purposes, made holy, useful to the Master and prepared to do any good work.*
>
> 2 TIMOTHY 2:20-21

John draws a direct distinction between listening to God and listening to the world when he says:

> *You, dear children, are from God and have overcome them, because the one who is in you is greater than the one who is in the world. They are from the world and therefore speak from the viewpoint of the world, and the world listens to them. We are from God, and whoever knows God listens to us; but whoever is not from God does not listen to us. This is how we recognize the Spirit of truth and the spirit of falsehood.*
>
> 1 JOHN 4:4-6

James is very direct in pointing out what it means to be a friend of the world:

You adulterous people, don't you know that friendship with the world is hatred toward God? Anyone who chooses to be a friend of the world becomes an enemy of God.

JAMES 4:4

The lust of the eyes, lust of the flesh, and the pride of life are where all sin is rooted, and they are in direct opposition to the Scriptures. The world will hate the Christian as Jesus said in John 17:14:

I have given them your word and the world has hated them, for they are not of the world any more than I am of the world.

The world hates the Bible because they are in direct opposition to the Scriptures. If we are worldly, we are agreeing with the devil, which will destroy our faith, because instead of trusting in God's provision, healing, etc., we trust the world. So the testing that Jesus went through, we all go through to see whom we trust, or what we trust. Do we trust the Lord and his Word or do we trust the devil and the world? Throughout our time on earth we are constantly being tested in a wide range of issues, but all sin comes down to our attachment to the world and the lust of the eyes, lust of the flesh, and the pride of life.

ꙮ **God tests for sin:**

"Therefore this is what the LORD Almighty says. See, I will refine and test them, for what else can I do because of the sin of my people?"

JEREMIAH 9:7.

- **God tests to see if you love him:**

  "The LORD your God is testing you to find out whether you love him with all your heart and with all your soul."

  DEUTERONOMY 13:3

- **God tests to see if you fear him:**

  Moses said to the people, "Do not be afraid. God has come to test you, so that the fear of God will be with you to keep you from sinning."

  EXODUS 20:20.

- **God tests to bring forth purity:**

  "But he knows the way that I take; when he has tested me, I will come forth as gold."

  JOB 23:10

- **God tests to see if you will follow his instructions:**

  "Then the Lord said to Moses, 'I will rain down bread from Heaven for you. The people are to go out each day and gather enough for that day. In this way I will test them and see whether they will follow my instructions'."

  EXODUS 16:4

- **God tests you to see what is in your heart:**

  "Remember how the LORD your God led you all the way in the wilderness these forty years, to humble and test you in order to know what was in your heart."

  DEUTERONOMY 8:2

If Satan has a stronghold in any area of our lives from an attachment to the world, we must get rid of it that we may walk in the fullness of the anointing. The closer we are to walking as Jesus walked, the more effective we will be in signs, wonders, and miracles. We don't want to operate in miracles without love; we want to operate in miracles because of love.

Every Christian has something to build in himself and in his calling (assignment), and we must build properly. If not built properly then what has been built will collapse. Jesus says:

> *Why do you call me, "Lord, Lord," and do not do what I say? As for everyone who comes to me and hears my words and puts them into practice, I will show you what they are like. They are like a man building a house, who dug down deep and laid the foundation on rock.*
>
> *When a flood came, the torrent struck that house but could not shake it, because it was well built. But the one who hears my words and does not put them into practice is like a man who built a house on the ground without a foundation. The moment the torrent struck that house, it collapsed and its destruction was complete.*
>
> LUKE 6:46-49

There are two types of service, one that would say "Lord, Lord," but not really be known by God; and the other that knows God and has minimized worldly attachments. One ministry honors self, and the other honors God. The tests we encounter will prepare us for signs, wonders, and miracles, as our hearts' cry is "God prepare me for serving you."

Simon the sorcerer followed Philip and was astonished by the great signs and miracles that he saw; consequently, he believed and was baptized (Acts 8:13).

However, Peter recognized something in him and said to Simon:

> *You have no part or share in this ministry, because your heart is not right before God. Repent of this wickedness and pray to the Lord in the hope that he may forgive you for having such a thought in your heart. For I see that you are full of bitterness and captive to sin.*
>
> ACTS 8:21-23

Although Simon believed and was baptized, Peter said that Simon had "no part or share in this ministry." Simon was full of bitterness and captive to sin, and consequently disqualified from relevant ministry. The sin in his life had a hold on him that disqualified him from serving God.

The pattern that Jesus followed as he entered his ministry is the pattern that every Christian must somewhat expect, as they seek to serve God.

Every Christian can heal the sick, but because you can heal the sick doesn't mean that you are super spiritual, or even going to Heaven. Everything we do as Christians hinges on our love for Jesus.

THE HARVEST FIELD

In some towns, there seems to be a church on every corner. Do we, perhaps, have too many churches? Jesus didn't think so. In fact, he said this to his disciples:

> *The harvest is plentiful but the workers are few. Ask the Lord of the harvest, therefore, to send out workers into his harvest field.*
>
> MATTHEW 9:37-38

Jesus said that there were not enough workers to work a plentiful harvest field. The Lord is asking his disciples to pray for laborers to be sent out into the harvest field. This actually means to force out laborers into the harvest field. There is no shortage of ministry opportunities. The shortage is in the number of workers who do the things that Jesus did.

The question is this: what kind of laborers would Jesus prefer to have in the harvest field? Without a doubt, it would be those who model the ministry that Jesus modeled, and that is preaching, teaching and healing the sick.

If the poor economy and high unemployment continue, the number of people needing help will increase. God is preparing the harvest field as he did in the time of the patriarchs in Egypt.

> *He called down famine on the land and destroyed all their supplies of food; and he sent a man before them—Joseph, sold as a slave.*
> PSALM 105:16-17

If you're forced out into the harvest field, do you think you will be able to heal the sick, raise the dead, cleanse the leper, and drive out demons? Yes, we all can do that. God wants to force us out of our comfort zone into the harvest field, and as you begin to take steps of faith, you also can enter that *"greater things"* ministry.

When God sees you, he sees the potential in you and where he wants to take you. The angel of the Lord saw Gideon and called him *"mighty warrior,"* even though at the time he was far from that (Judges 6:11-13).

God is speaking to people of this day and calling them out to be mighty warriors. Gideon had trouble believing that he was a "mighty warrior" in spite of what the angel of the Lord said. You don't thresh wheat in a winepress; you press wine. He was in the winepress hiding from the Midianites.

The Midianites would raid the Israelites and steal their crops and kill their animals. Some of us in the modern church today are like Gideon, not wanting to step out of our comfort zone.

You may not feel like a mighty warrior, but in Christ that is exactly what you can be. It's wrong for Christians to sit out the war that is going on. The battle (spiritual) is raging all around on many fronts, and we must keep in mind, *"faith without works is dead."* God wants you in the harvest field, not sitting home watching TV.

There are many Scriptures in the Bible that commission Christians for ministry. One such commission was after the death and burial of Jesus. The disciples were hiding behind locked doors for fear of the Jews, not fully knowing what happened to the Lord, when "Jesus came and stood among them and said:

> *"Peace be with you! As the Father has sent me, I am sending you." And with that he breathed on them and said, "Receive the Holy Spirit. If you forgive anyone his sins, they are forgiven; if you do not forgive them, they are not forgiven."*
>
> JOHN 20:21-23

We have been breathed on and sent, and if we are reluctant, then God will force us out of our comfort zone to get us into the harvest field. There are times when we all need a little forcing.

The end-time harvest will take miracles. Be assured there is power in his Word, power in his name, and power in the Holy Ghost. These are available for every Christian—no exceptions.

APPENDIX A
TESTIMONIES

They triumphed over him by the blood of the Lamb and by the word of their testimony ...
REVELATION 12:11A

Paul ministered at our church—Restoration World Outreach with Drs. John & Rebecca Polis—in Asheville and prayed for our grandson, Noah. He had asthma so severe he had been hospitalized three times in one year. He went forward and after that prayer he has been totally healed and loves to testify what God did in his life. He is 10 years old. Thanks for your faithfulness and know we are standing in the gap for the Costa family.

—Dean & Margaret Poteat

I was a visitor to the World Lighthouse Worship Center in Grantsville, Maryland. Paul was an amazingly yielded vessel. My husband and I have attended some wonderful meetings in the past where the Spirit of the Lord moved in healing and prophecy but we were both in amazement in the humility it took to say "Pastor, call some people up here," instead of just him moving in his gifting for whoever he felt the Lord was leading him to speak to. This was a real blessing to see. Deferring to the leadership blessed that church.

Paul did a healing line and just sat and held people's feet (HUMILITY) and prayed such simple prayers of faith. MANIFESTATIONS came, God was glorified and people were set free, delivered, and healed. WOW. There was no loud music playing; there was no "hoopla" just the manifested presence of the living God.

—Grantville, MD

I have suffered from plantar fasciatis in both of my feet since the birth of our last child, 2 1/2 months to be exact. Severe pain at times, all the time. After Paul prayed, it is TOTALLY GONE! I'm still having symptoms of allergies, but I am no longer labeling them "my____." I'm believing God for healing and waiting to see it manifested. I'm rebuking the enemy and deeply desiring now to seek out the Scriptures on healing for a more clear understanding of God's heart and God's will.

Paul's ministry at Harvest Fellowship Church today in Leedey, Oklahoma was amazing. I so apprecated the simple, no hype way of ministering the love of God to His people! Many people were healed, and the prophetic words were right on. They were words in due season that put the wind of the Lord back in our sails! We love Paul, and pray God's abundant blessings over him, his family, and his ministry.

—Pastor Mark & Jada Haney

Paul Costa is a man of God who walks in great humility and with anointing to minister life to the people of God. His administration of the true gift of prophecy has been an incredible blessing to our congregation, and notable healings take place in every service. One of the greatest things to be said about Paul's ministry is this: when the services are over, the people leave with their eyes on the power and grace of God and not on man. Our church has been truly blessed by the ministry of Paul Costa.

—Pastor Steve Payne

We just had Paul Costa here with us in the "Northeast Kingdom" of Vermont for a time of ministry. He is definitely one of those voices which speaks into the life of a ministry, church, town, and region that will make a definite difference in the spiritual climate.

Paul's personal ministry in healing and the prophetic is growing in depth and accuracy. The Lord spoke much through Paul to individuals, leaders, and the pastors that was both confirming and challenging. Paul's ministry is that of a Kingdom builder. His apostolic insight is powerful and definitely has a handle on territorial issues in the spirit.

To know that Paul Costa is part of an international team of apostles with Dr. John Kelly, C. Peter Wagner, and others, and yet is humble enough to come to smaller churches like ours is a huge blessing. His down to earth style and eagerness to minister to us personally was appreciated.

—Pastors Rick & Carmen Menard

We have had the great privilege of receiving the ministry of Dr. Paul Costa on two occasions now, and we have witnessed astounding demonstrations of the Holy Spirit's power during both visits. Standing six-foot-five, Dr. Costa is a "gentle giant" who carries a dynamic ministry anointing which manifests itself in the form of dramatic and often instantaneous miracles. As the Apostle Paul stated in his letter to the church at Corinth, *"Truly the signs of an apostle were accomplished among you with all perseverance, in signs and wonders and mighty deeds"* (2 Cor. 12:12).

With no exaggeration, I can confidently say that these same signs and wonders were evident in Dr. Costa's ministry here at the Antioch Church of New England. Legs, hips, necks, backs, arthritis, heart problems and many other ailments were healed. Reports of life-changing miracles are still coming in. Greatest of all, souls were won to the Lord Jesus Christ and many rededicated their lives to the Lord's service.

Dr. Costa's teachings were truly apostolic; his prophetic words over our people were right on target; and a mighty evangelistic anointing flowed as he shared his life story, even bringing grown men to tears. Dr. Costa is a true shepherd and loving spiritual father to many and I highly recommend his ministry to anyone who is hungry to witness the fruits of the apostolic restoration that is currently taking place in the Body of Christ world-wide. If I could describe Dr. Costa's ministry with one word, it would be this—powerful.

—Pastor K.D. Anderholm

We were delighted to have Apostle Paul Costa with us here at The Eagle's Nest and Eagle's Flight Ministries in Waycross, Georgia. So very often we have seen ministers pass through our area who have little regard for anything other than a paycheck. We were hungry to see integrity in ministry. When Paul stood up to speak, the Holy Spirit began to move in a most extraordinary way. We saw many healed and set free from bondage of the enemy. Hes messages were strong, anointed, and to the point. I believe the best way to summarize what we saw and experienced would be this: "That's the real deal!"

We are excited about our relationship with this man of God who will not come to use or abuse you, but rather pour out the anointing of healing and the prophetic the Lord has gifted him with.

—Dr. Randy Pelka

Paul Costa is one of the best prophetic leaders I've ever known. Very few prophetic voices in the twenty-first century have his combination of gifts, character, background, and leadership. I am completely unreserved in recommending Paul Costa's ministry because I know him well. I trust his walk with the Lord, his counsel, and his apostolic service to the Kingdom of God. I believe Paul Costa is being used by God as a voice to the trans-local and trans-national body at this breakthrough time in the Church.

—Pastor Tim Triplett

We believe that, in our journey with God, there are crossroads in which the Lord sovereignly joins us with those who will help us fulfill our divine destiny. Three years ago, we met such a man in Dr. Paul Costa. His ministry has pulled back the curtains into the heavens that we might see the heavenly pattern for our local assembly.

The Spirit of God has truly used him to unveil the gifts, ministries, and potential within our people at Jubilee Ministries. Each time he has visited our church, he has helped us to climb into new levels of the Spirit. Dr. Costa's ministry has helped us develop and equip our ministry that we might impact our region. We have been truly blessed by the prophetic mantle on this man of God's life as he ministers over the lives of our congregation with great accuracy.

Personally, he has been a companion in tribulation as he has helped my family and me through trying times. To sum up the ministry of Dr. Costa, if you were to shine a flashlight on his heart, it would shine through his back with the same intensity because of the transparency of his life. Since the time we've crossed paths we have become more fruitful in our lives and ministry because of this man of God.

—Pastors Mark & Jill Kauffman

Paul Costa ministered at Catskill Mountain Christian Center, Margaretville, New York where his presentation was mature, prophetic, and practical as he convincingly cast a vision for the church's purpose as being a vehicle of transformation. Costa showed that this transformation should include our personal lives as well as our churches, communities, and the world.

Paul is an articulate spokesman for the apostolic movement and is very capable in the gifts of prophecy and healing. He prayed for many of our people with excellent prophetic accuracy and skill, and his healing prayer resulted in several notable healings. Paul operated flawlessly under the covering of local church leadership, building up the church within the context of our vision and protocol. I wholeheartedly recommend Paul Costa's ministry.

—Pastor Bob Engelhardt

Paul Costa came to us as a result of a high recommendation from a trusted brother in Christ. From the very first visit, Paul endeared himself to the congregation. They were put at ease by his humility which then enabled him to be honored by the Presence of the Lord.

The prophetic utterances were clear, punctual, and precise. The church witnessed many fulfillments of these utterances, some within a few days. During the same services, Paul manifested the gift of healing. Many were touched deeply by the miraculous work of the Lord.

We have had the pleasure of Paul ministering to us for three consecutive years. There is an expectation in the people as he continues to return and build this local house. Paul Costa has become a friend and covenant brother to us personally as well as a fellow builder in the Body of Christ. We would recommend him to those who are serious about the maturity of the church and advancing the Kingdom of God.

—Living Word Christian Church, Greenville, PA
Pastor Jim Chapin

Paul always prays for the sick when he ministers in churches, but he does it in such a low key manner that we sometimes take it for granted. He has an incredibly high rate of success in healing, and on many occasions it's been 100% (as reported by others). Paul simply says, "That's what is supposed to happen," and gives all the glory to the Lord.

Paul ministered at Living Word Christian Church in three meetings without praying for the sick (at the request of Pastor Jim who just wanted all people to get a prophetic word for 2006). Jim later told Paul about a lady who gave a testimony the following Sunday. She had asked Paul to pray for her when she came up for a prophetic word—she was deaf in one ear. She said that her hearing was restored, and her knee was healed, which she hadn't even mentioned to Paul.

—Living Word Christian Church, Greenville, PA
Pastor Jan Chapin

In the second meeting that Paul ministered in, a tearful mother told Paul that her son, who had been a hunchback, was healed.

—Bible Truth Apostolic Church, El Campo, TX
Pastor Larry Smith

A young lady who had been in a car accident came up for prayer. She had bandages on her head, arm, and leg, and as she hobbled up it was obvious she was in a great deal of pain. She was healed and walked back to her seat pain free, and without a limp. That same month Paul had a similar situation with another girl who had been in a car accident, and she was healed.

—Full Gospel Chapel, Avoca, PA
Dwayne Mitchell

A lady testified that last year when Paul ministered at the church, he asked for a show of hands of those that were healed during the meeting. He then asked for those who didn't get healed to raise their hands, and the lady raised her hand (the only hand that went up). She said that she had arthritis in both hands and her fingers were deformed. She was healed later in the day, and her fingers were all straightened out, and she had full use of her hand, which she didn't have before!

—Masters Hand Christian Fellowship, New Rochelle, NY
Pastor Terry Noschese

A lady came up for prayer during the ministry time, and wanted Paul to pray for her granddaughter. The little girl had been born with a shriveled hand, which she had never been able to use. Paul prayed and agreed with the grandmother. The grandmother immediately called her son and he said that very instant, the girl reached and grabbed something for the first time in her life.

—Harvest Fellowship Church, Leedey, OK
Pastors Mark & Jada Haney

APPENDIX B

Paul Costa's Testimony

They triumphed over him by the blood of the Lamb and by the word of their testimony ...

Revelation 12:11a

My most memorable year in my pro football career was my sixth year. I had been a tight end for 4 years (playing in the pro bowl twice), then was moved to offensive tackle. My sixth season playing offensive tackle was my best year in pro football. I was looking forward to playing a lot of years of pro ball at that position; it was easy compared to playing tight end. A tight end had to run pass patterns, then on the next play he had to block at the point of attack. You would move from left side to the right of the formation and do a lot of different blocks and patterns; but a tackle has his little piece of ground, and although the action is intense, it's a lot easier than playing tight end and running all over the field. The personal combat that you have is kind of a fun thing to do. I could picture myself doing that for a lot of years.

But something happened that off season that completely changed my life. It was a Sunday in April that my 4 ½-year-old son had been taken to the hospital by ambulance. I was called and told that I should get to the hospital as soon as I could. So I got in my Corvette convertible and zipped up the west side of Buffalo to Children's Hospital. I was told to go to the second floor and the nurse there said that it was very serious and that he probably would not make it. In my thinking, there was no way I could believe that something could happen to my son. He was the most precious thing in my life. The doctor came up a little while later, and told me that my son had died in intensive care of complications from childhood Leukemia. It was a sudden thing; something that we didn't expect. I cursed God on the second floor of Buffalo Children's Hospital because I blamed Him. I didn't know God, but I blamed Him anyway

I blamed God for a few months until I came to the same reasoning that King David had when his son died. David had a relationship with Bathsheba and had a son from that relationship who was dying. David was in sackcloth and ashes and praying that God would spare his son, but his son died. Afterwards, David got up and bathed and cleaned himself up and his servants were puzzled about this and they asked him, "Why now do you get cleaned up and want to eat?" David said, "I can't bring my son back but I can go to him." That was the way I was picturing things. I really wanted to go to Heaven to see my son but I didn't know how to get there and I didn't know who to ask. I had a friend who was a man of the cloth and I used to go drinking with him so I asked him. I said, "Kevin, how do I go to Heaven—I want to go to Heaven when I die." He said, "Don't worry about it; all you have to do is treat people right and you'll go to Heaven." I thought, "That's pretty easy; I'll try to be a good guy from now on," but after a year or two of trying to be good and treat people right, I knew that I was failing. I thought to myself, "There's no way I can go to Heaven." I even had people tell me, "You know, you're not a very good person; you're kinda mean."

I lost all desire to play professional football. It became like any mundane job—like punching a time clock. I can remember standing on the sidelines on game day with all the hoopla that's going on at a professional game—all the media, celebrity types, etc.—I'd be standing on the sidelines while they were playing *The Star Bangled Banner,* looking up at the gray Buffalo sky, thinking to myself, "What am I doing here; wearing this stupid uniform, playing this stupid game?" I could not make heads or tails at what I was doing.

I played 4 more years of football after that, but it was difficult because all the real fire and passion for the game was gone. It was something that I went out and did because it was a job. After 8 years in Buffalo, I retired; I just couldn't do it any more. A year after retirement, the World Football League started up and I was recruited to go to Birmingham, Alabama to play for the Birmingham Americans. I thought it would be a nice change of scenery for me with a nice climate and it would be an easy brand of football and a lot of fun. So, I moved to Birmingham, Alabama and I met some guys on the team that were really weird. There were some young players who were telling me that they had a personal relationship with God. I thought, "Man that is cosmic. That is so bizarre to have a relationship with God. That is so way out."

Denny Duron was a young player whom the coach would always call on to pray before games and he prayed beautiful prayers. I would think to myself, "How does he make all that stuff up about God? That is wild; where did he get all this? I have to get this on a tape recorder." Denny and I struck up a relationship and I remember when we were playing in Hawaii, he said, "Paul, how about taking a ride around the island with me?" I thought to myself, "Cool; I've got nothing better to do than take a ride." so I went with this preacher's kid, who was a quarterback, and was taking pictures of him at all of these little churches around the island. I was the biggest pagan on the team and when I got back, I began wondering, "Man, what am I doing? Am I cracking up? What is this all about?" This guy has one foot in Heaven and I've got one foot in Hell and we've got nothing in common and here I am, riding around the island with this guy.

One night, Denny was going to preach at a church in Birmingham and he asked me to go. I thought I had nothing better to do so I'd go listen to what he had to say; maybe it would be interesting and if not, I could always skip out. Anyway, the bars don't really get going until later so I thought I'd go check it out. I got to the church late and as I walked across the church parking lot, I could see a guy standing at the church door with a stack of papers under his arm. He was looking at me like I was the only one there. My first impression when I saw the papers is that he was going to try to sell me some insurance.

When I got to the door, he said, "Hey brother, how are you?" and he handed me a bulletin. I went into the large sanctuary and the church was packed with about 1,200 people. They were in the middle of praise and worship and had their hands raised and praising God. I thought to myself, "These people are weird; I've got to get out of here in a hurry." I turned around to leave and saw the guy that I thought was an insurance salesman still standing at the door. He smiled at me and waved and I thought, "I'm trapped," so I looked for a place to sit and the only empty seat I could find was on the second row. I walked up there and a teammate of mine, Calvin Miller, was standing there. I thought, "Great, here's a player in the same boat that I was in; I'll go and sit with him."

Calvin Miller played for the NY Giants when he left the WFL and the NY Press called him "Killer Miller." I sat next to Calvin and felt relieved that I knew someone who was as uncomfortable there as I was. There was a family sitting in front of us with about four kids, right off the farm, raising their hands and praising God and speaking in tongues, which I thought was Latin. I thought, "Look at these hayseeds, speaking Latin. I went to Notre Dame and I can't even speak Latin."

Then the pastor comes out. I really didn't like this guy at all. At first glance, he came on stage with his patent leather shoes, and his three-piece pastel green suit. Every hair was in place and he had one of those Pentecostal pompadours. In perfect diction, he said, "I want every person here to hold hands with the person next to them." There I was—holding Killer Miller's hand, thinking to myself, "I've got to get out of here." It was weird; it was a strange experience because I didn't have any understanding that you can have a genuine relationship with God. I had no understanding that people truly have a desire to worship and praise the Living God.

I left that night and it didn't make a dent in me. I was more determined than ever to stay away from places like that. I thought it would be a bad influence on me and I didn't ever want to go to a place like that again. But you know what happened about a month later? I was driving down a street in my gold Mercedes Benz and all of a sudden, I knew beyond a shadow of a doubt, that I had to get right with God—right then. I had no idea what to do. As I was driving up the main drag in Homewood, Alabama, there was a church on my left and I thought I'd find someone there and I'd bring them before the altar and have them introduce me to God. The door was open and I went halfway down the aisle, but I couldn't find anyone and didn't know what to do. I sat down on a pew and knelt down and gave my life to God. The Bible says, *"Believe in your heart and confess with your mouth, and you will be saved."* That's what I did in my own awkward way because I didn't have any idea how to do it and didn't have anyone to lead me.

Several days later, I went to a chapel service before a game and Denny was talking about a born-again experience. I thought, "Hey, I did that."

I told my teammates later that I was a born-again Christian. I had been so bad that no one believed me. I had to convince all of them that I was serious. That week was when I realized the impact of what I had done and how important it was. When the guys finally believed me, they said, "Paul, God is going to change your life, because if anyone is in Christ, he is a new creation; the old has gone and the new has come." Denny gave me a Bible, and as part of the inscription he wrote, "May the Word of God change your priorities and perspectives." That really puzzled me at the time because I didn't know the Word of God could change anybody and I thought if I were going to change, then I would have to do the changing. But, I got in the Word, and I saw as time passed, how sinful things began to leave. I really was quite excited; so excited about my relationship with God.

Going back to my boyhood, one of the things I remember all my life was wanting something eternal. Anytime I would get something new, like a new toy, or a new car, I would think to myself that it had no worth because it wasn't eternal. If I got something for Christmas, I'd think, "This is nice but it's not eternal and has no lasting meaning or purpose." Now all of a sudden, I had something eternal. You can't imagine how excited I was.

When the WFL folded, we moved to Springfield, Missouri where I helped Denny Duron coach football on a volunteer basis at Evangel College. This was a brand new freshman team, playing varsity football. There I was, right out of professional football, coaching at Evangel College. Our first game was against William Jewel. It wasn't the Eagles; it wasn't the Giants or the Cowboys; but William Jewell. Instead of having thousands of fans and hundreds of press covering the game, we had a handful of parents and students. I looked across the field on game day at these young players thinking, "We can't lose to William Jewel," but we lost. It was a weird experience because one thing I said I would never do was coach football. God has a wonderful way of making me eat crow because when I got saved, there were a lot of things I said I'd never do that I ended up doing.

The Bible says in Joel 2:25, that the Lord will restore the years the locusts have eaten. That verse was never more true when, on February 8, 1978, our son Clark was born. I knew that I would never see my son, Paul again on this earth but when Clark was born, it was like having 2 sons in one. I was totally amazed when I looked at Clark for the first time and realized how much God loved me when He blessed me with him.

One day I was driving down the highway outside of Springfield, and the Spirit of God filled my car. I have never experienced this again. I've experienced things close to this but not the way the Spirit of God filled my car that day. God spoke to my heart as clear as a bell and He said, "I'm calling you into the ministry and I'm sending you back to your hometown." I went back to Port Chester, NY as a new Christian but through God, our congregation grew every Sunday for a year and a half. I didn't have a clue what I was doing. My ministry back then was like throwing mud on a wall. If it stuck, I'd use it; if it didn't stick, I wouldn't. Then I'd read a book or hear a minister say, "We're a New Testament Church," but no one had any idea back then what a New Testament Church was. There were so many mistakes being made in the local church, it's not surprising the number of casualties and failures we had. It's just this day that we're beginning to have this understanding and things are being restructured for the purpose of God. It had to happen. The greatest revival the world has ever seen has hit and is about to spread across the world in areas that have been dead for so long.

What we see that went on in South Korea in the 80s and is now in Nigeria and parts of Africa, is going to spread throughout the world. Why? Because Jesus said, *"All authority has been given to me in Heaven and earth; therefore, go and make disciples of all nations."* That's not on His wish list. He just didn't say that because it's an encouraging thing to say to His people, but it is a prophetic declaration of victory—a prophetic declaration of war that we're going to carry out as the Body of Christ in filling the earth with the glory of God.

My dad died a number of years ago and the last few years of his life were pretty depressing because he had an aneurysm, a leg amputated, kidney failure, heart trouble, and numerous other problems. I was pastoring in Birmingham, Alabama and Mom called me to come home because my father was very ill and they didn't think he would survive. I got to the hospital and while I'm walking to his room, I hear him talking to his nurse and he was very animated and happy. When I walked into his room, he said, "Buster, you'll never guess what happened to me last night. The Lord took me to Heaven and some angels took me in a room and drained all of my blood and filled me with the blood of Jesus. The Lord kept speaking to me and saying, 'Just follow me.' The Lord told me I wasn't going to die now but I would die soon." My father could not wait to die. He said Heaven was so beautiful that it was unimaginable. He told my mother, "Molly, I want you to die with me" (but she declined). He wanted all his kids to die with him except me; he said that I had to stay here to do the Lord's work. Then he told me that I'd really taught him right and that he'd never forget me for leading him the right way. I was hoping he wouldn't forget me any way since I was his oldest son. He was so excited that when he died a few months later, I was ecstatic for him.

That's the way God is—the glorious King of Kings and the Lord of Lords. I remember being a young Christian, standing under a beautiful starlit night and I was praying, looking at the stars above. It was a perfectly clear night and I said, "Lord, if you love me, show me a shooting star." Exactly where I was looking and exactly when I said that, a shooting star went across the sky. I kind of forgot about it until a few years later when I was on a beach on Long Island with my son, Clark and my wife, Jan. They were back at the house where we were staying and I took a walk to look at the beautiful night sky and stars. And I said, "Lord, remember the time you showed me the shooting star? I haven't a shadow of a doubt that you showed it to me but just to prove to me that it wasn't a coincidence, would you show me another shooting star?" And just as soon as I said that, another shooting star went across the sky. I looked and looked for other shooting stars but saw nothing. But then I got real brazen. I stepped up to the water's edge and said, "Lord, I know that those shooting stars weren't accidents but would you just prove to me beyond a shadow of a doubt that you sent it and send another shooting star?" And exactly where I was looking, another shooting star went across the sky.

Now, how does God do these things? Does he wake up in the morning and think, "My goodness, let's see what Costa is doing. He's a mess; let me go down there and straighten things out." No, from the very foundation of the world, He said, "I'm going to put in Paul Costa's heart to ask me to show him a shooting star in such and such a year; such and such a month, week, day, hour, minute, second. I'm going to start that star from the very foundation of the world. Then I'm going to put it in his heart again this year, this month, right down to the very second, to ask me for another shooting star." Why does God do stuff like that? For the same reason He sent His Son to the cross for us—because He loves us.

230 | *Healing* THE MULTITUDES

Paul Costa makes a spectacular catch against Boston to keep an important drive alive—November 7, 1965

Photo by Robert L. Smith, Photographer for the Buffalo Bills

ABOUT THE AUTHOR
MEET PAUL COSTA

Dr. Paul Costa has been in the ministry for over 30 years. Sixteen of those years he pastored churches. He now travels and ministers worldwide. Paul holds a B.A. degree from the University of Notre Dame and M.A and Ph.D. degrees from the California Graduate School of Theology.

After graduation from Notre Dame, Costa played professional football for 10 years: 8 years with the Buffalo Bills and 2 years in the World Football League. Paul won a starting job at tight-end his rookie year with the Bills and soon became one of the premier tight-ends in the AFL, playing in 2 Pro Bowls. He moved to offensive tackle in his fifth year with the Bills and became a standout, making All Pro in his second year as a tackle. Costa played with such notables as Jack Kemp and O.J. Simpson.

Besides having a strong pulpit ministry, Paul is powerfully gifted in healing, miracles, and the prophetic. There are always numerous testimonies of dramatic healings in all of his meetings. His prophetic gift will release the saints of God into functional ministry. Paul is passionate about raising up leaders to fulfill their calling and impacting the world around them.

Costa has been a guest on various Christian TV and radio venues. He was the editor of *The Networker*, a cutting-edge apostolic/prophetic magazine for Christian leaders, and has also co-authored several books with Apostle John Kelly (such as *End Time Warriors*, and *The Power to Get Wealth*).

Paul and his wife, Jan have one son, Clark, who lives in Grapevine, Texas with his wife, Alexis.

WWW.PAULCOSTAMINISTRY.COM
EMAIL: SPAULCOSTA@GMAIL.COM

AVAILABLE ON amazon.com

PLEASE LEAVE US A REVIEW OR TESTIMONY

1. Go to amazon.com.
2. Search for **Healing the Multitudes** by Paul Costa.
3. Scroll all the way to the bottom and click on the button, "**Write a Customer Review**."
4. Rate the book (out of 5 stars) and write your review.
5. Submit.

Note: You do not have to purchase the book on amazon to leave a review. Anyone with an amazon account is eligible to write a review for any book they have read.

Thank You!

www.ingramcontent.com/pod-product-compliance
Lightning Source LLC
LaVergne TN
LVHW051548070426
835507LV00021B/2473